Fabian Vogt

Luther on the Fly

Translated by
Christian Rendel

Fabian Vogt

LUTHER
on the
FLY

His Most Important
Writings in a Nutshell

edition chrismon

Bibliographic information published by the Deutsche
Nationalbibliothek
The Deutsche Nationalbibliothek lists this publication in the Deutsche
Nationalbiographie; detailed bibliographic data are available on the
internet at http://dnb.dnb.de.

Cover: Hansisches Druck- und Verlagshaus, Frankfurt a. M., Anja Haß
Coverillustration: Oliver Weiss, Berlin
Innengestaltung und Satz: Makena Plangrafik, Leipzig
Druck und Binden: BELTZ Bad Langensalza GmbH

ISBN 978-3-96038-086-3

www.eva-leipzig.de

'STAND UP FIRMLY,
SPEAK UP CLEARLY,
SHUT UP EARLY.'

Martin Luther

PREFACE

Can words change the world? Of course they can! No one has given more impressive proof of that than Martin Luther, the courageous, uncompromising and passionate 16th century Reformer who became one of the founders of the modern age with his daring writings.

At the end of the Middle Ages, Luther demonstrated the unbelievable explosive force of words. The history of the Reformation is an example of the way rousing phrases can, under certain conditions, shake up a society more thoroughly than new laws, amazing technologies or entire armies – and how easily a person with imagination can jump into another, better world with a single leap.

It is no surprise, then, that some of Luther's writings have been added to the UNESCO Memory of the World Programme. They tell the fascinating story of a plucky monk who successfully took up the fight with all the powers that were at his time – the pope, the Emperor, the nobility and with all who were – in his opinion – adhering to a wrong and life-stifling way of thinking.

But Luther did not fight with a sword. His weapons were words, written as well as spoken, loud as well as soft, erudite as well as provocative and polemic, deadly serious as well as full of jest. A mighty wielder of words, the unconventional thinker from Wittenberg called the ruling system in question until no one could get away from his outrageous outspokenness. The result was the Reformation, a great 'process of renewal of the Christian faith' – and with it came a far-reaching transformation of church and state whose beneficial after-effects we still feel today. Thank God!

Thus, the best way to get familiar and understand Martin Luther's importance is to get to know and understand his great writings: those trailblazing publications that topped the 16th century bestseller lists for years, even decades, although they were not called that at the time.

The book you are holding in your hands now will introduce you to typical examples from Luther's most important writings in a way that is short and to the point, accessible and easy to understand, informative and highly entertaining. It will serve you an array of 'Lutheran' appetizers, as it were, a kind of Wittenberg starter plate. With only the best ingredients of course: from the famed '95 Theses' to 'On the Freedom of a Christian' to Luther's speech at the Diet of Worms which made it irrevocably clear that this celebrated popular hero was fundamentally challenging the way the world was ordered.

My hope is that after reading this book, you will not only have discovered what made – and makes – this extraordinary spiritual awakening so very powerful, but also acquired a taste for relating the explosiveness of some of Luther's revolutionary statements to our everyday life in the 21st century. Join the discussion!

Besides, wouldn't it be nice to be able to let your profound knowledge of history shine through at parties and receptions from now on? 'Oh, it's interesting that you say that. By the way, Martin Luther wisely remarked something very like that in his „Open Letter on Translating" ...' But no ... you would never stoop so low of course.

I am convinced that it is wholesome to talk about Luther and the things he has to say to us. For the Reformer's wisdom still inspires us today and invites us to look with curiosity and discernment at seemingly immovable structures and fixed habits. Or, as the later Reformers themselves put it with respect to the theological impulses of their movement: 'Ecclesia semper reformanda!' – The church is always in need of reformation. In other words, the change must never stop.

If that is true, then it must have been clear to Luther from the beginning that every one of us is called to contribute to this renewal. At least he once wrote: *The Church needs a reformation. But this reformation is not only the pope's or the cardinals' responsibility. It is the responsibility of the whole of Christendom, or even better, of God alone. Only he knows the hour of reformation.*

This means that if you start thinking about Luther, you will find yourself encouraged to become part of the ongoing process of Reformation. Maybe it was just this suggestive invitation to become a 'revolutionary of love' yourself that made his writing so luminous.

Before introducing you to a selection of Luther's writings, I would like to take you on an excursion into his writing workshop to take a look at the circumstances in which this diverse body of work came into being.

In a second introductory chapter, I then want to take you through the most significant stages of his life, for in the case of this Wittenberg professor it is highly instructive to be aware of the biographical background of his writings and to be able to relate them to the history of the Reformation.

After that, I will dare tackle twelve of Martin Luther's works and writings considered by scholars as milestones of Reformation history, giving you a highly condensed overview of their most important statements and concerns. In a nutshell, as it were, or compact, to use a modern expression.

This is a risk, of course. I know that well. Especially as I am taking the liberty of summarizing the texts. And summarizing always entails leaving things out. It entails bundling information and elementarizing. But that doesn't matter, I think. 500 years ago, after all, Luther himself was keen on making complex matters understandable for everyone. And if this gives you an appetite for reading the original work in its entirety – go for it! It's worth it.

This book, though, is called 'Luther on the Fly' – and for good reason. For reading Luther in the original is not a quick affair. Believe me! I have tried that thoroughly. Therefore, allow me to occasionally simplify, paraphrase or otherwise illustrate the theological connotations. Luther himself once described this approach thus: *If you preach about the article of justification, people will sleep and cough; but if you start offering stories and examples, they will perk up both ears and listen diligently.* Doesn't that sound encouraging?

Incidentally: For centuries, scholars have been trying to give an account of how Martin Luther might have managed to set so many people in motion in his time. What was his secret? Well, aside from the fact that we know today that the great reviver did have a dark side too and was, in the end, only one piece in the great jigsaw puzzle of the Reformation – albeit a pretty big one and most of all the one who got the whole thing started – it probably was his personality that contributed a lot to his life's work.

Put another way: Behind almost everything Luther ever published lay a personal life experience. Most of all the experience of a man driven by the fear of hell who suddenly discovered the freedom of heaven – a God-seeker who experienced the leap from primordial fear to a primal sense of trust as a personal new birth.

And as the Church of his time had not been able to help him in his desperate wrestling with his fears (it rather did the opposite), Luther took it upon himself to renew this institution. By doing that, he called ancient hierarchies into question that also pertained to worldly structures of power.

What is essential, then, is that behind all these social upheavals there was the 'converted' Reformer's ardent desire to make the 'Good News' of the love and mercy of

God accessible to as many seekers as possible. Or, as he himself put it: *Making a sad, despondent person happy is more than conquering a kingdom.* In this, of course, Luther was closely emulating his model Jesus Christ, who also changed history by changing the hearts of people.

Thus, the Lutheran answer to my question at the beginning – 'Can words change the world?' – is really: 'Yes, because they can change people's hearts.' Well, if such a power dwells in written words, then it is a pleasure to interact with them.

Wishing you a stimulating read,
Fabian Vogt

CONTENTS

LUTHER AND HIS WRITINGS

The importance that writing had for Martin Luther is illustrated by a nice anecdote that people still like to tell about him:

When the Reformer had to hide on the Wartburg in the summer of 1521 after the Church had excommunicated him and the Emperor had laid a ban on him in the edict of Worms, which made him an outlaw, he frequently was under the impression, so it is told, that he was being pursued by demons and evil spirits.

One day as he was sitting at his desk working as usual, the devil himself suddenly appeared in his little cell, teasing and tempting the already despondent fugitive. In his fear and panic, Luther is said to have grabbed his inkpot – which seems the closest projectile he could find – and hurled it in rage at the satanic confuscator, thereby succeeding, it seems, to drive him away.

For centuries, the ink stain resulting from this throw, or some sort of ink stain anyway, has been preserved and looked after on the Wartburg for the benefit of visitors – just because it is such a charming anecdote to tell.

Luther himself, though, never claimed to have thrown that inkpot. His words that inspired others to invent this picturesque story were: *I drove the devil away with ink.* What a great phrase, isn't it? *I drove the devil away with ink.* What the Reformer meant, of course, were his writings. All the things he had committed to paper with pen and ink: his letters, open letters, lectures, sermons, pamphlets and translations.

To put it in modern and somewhat psychological terms: Luther manages through writing to canalize those things that profoundly concern, trouble and worry him. In other words, his writings were, among other things, a successful antidote against despair, a wholesome self-therapy. It is certainly not a bad approach to deal with one's challenges and temptations, as Luther sometimes called those dark moments, by sorting out all the seemingly menacing thoughts and turning them into sagacious publications.

Without reading too much into Luther's phrase about ink and the devil, it is certainly characteristic of his writings that, as mentioned above, one senses in every single line how personally their subject matter concerns him, how much he wrestled and existentially battled with questions that deeply mattered to the unintentional "instigator" himself.

If you look at the sheer volume of Luther's publications, you get an inkling how much these "devilish" intrigues must have haunted him: about 350 printed writings, hundreds of sermons, 2,500 letters and almost 7,000 after-dinner speeches have been documented. And we probably can hardly imagine how effective particularly his printed writings were in Germany at the time.

It's true! Experts estimate that in the twenties and thirties of the 16th century, the works of Luther made up the majority of all books sold. Any author's dream. One huge print run after another came out of the presses – a deluge of hotly demanded literature, augmented by a constant supply of unauthorised reprints.

Furthermore, by medieval standards the spiritual "reviver" can be called a media superstar. Luther was probably indeed the first celebrity in history to have their printed portrait circulating extensively in the whole Empire. Thus, from the North Sea coast down to Lake Constance, every woman and every man knew what the famous, rebellious theologian looked like. Something like that had never happened before.

In view of that it is true, of course, that Luther owed his breakthrough, among other things, to the relatively recent invention of book printing. Since Johannes Gutenberg had laid the foundation for modern book printing and invented the printing press in Mainz around 1450, it had become possible to copy and distribute texts in large numbers. Until then, every book had to be copied manually in a painstaking process that took months.

Nevertheless, this provided only the technological means for distribution. Another circumstance proved just as essential for the great resonance Luther's writings found: that he was able as a scholar, theologian and preacher to express himself in a clear, true-to-life and entertaining way. The things he published were plain-spoken, bold, challenging and highly eloquent at the same time. Luther had such an overwhelmingly impressive way with words that he left indelible marks in the German language. It is fair to say that Luther was one of the most important initiators of New High German.

Most people do not realize, for example, how many idiomatic phrases and figures of speech still prevalent today go back to Martin Luther: 'Hochmut kommt vor dem Fall' ('pride comes before the fall'), 'Wer anderen eine Grube gräbt, fällt selbst hinein' ('harm set, harm get'), 'Perlen vor die Säue werfen' ('casting pearls to the swine'), 'Im Dunkeln tappen' ('grope in the dark'), 'Die Haare zu Berge stehen haben' ('having one's hair stand on end'), 'Ein Buch mit sieben Siegeln' ('a book with seven seals') or 'Wer den Pfennig nicht ehrt, ist des Talers nicht wert' ('take care of the pennies, and the pounds will look after themselves'). Indeed, if it weren't for this creative reformer of language we would have to do without such glorious words as 'Bluthund' ('bloodhound'), 'Feuertaufe' ('baptism of fire'), 'Machtwort' (literally 'power word', an authoritative statement to settle a matter), 'Lockvogel' (literally 'luring bird', a decoy) and many others. And when he really got going, he could even get a little coarse, as for example with his famous saying, *From a sad arse comes no happy fart*. Graphic enough for you?

Luther had an extraordinary feeling for language, perhaps because he was himself a singer, played the lute and the flute, and as a poet over the years penned 36 hymns still known in our time. Songs whose lyrics full of fighting spirit contributed much to the spreading of the Reformation as they were a sort of pamphlets for the illiterate.

Furthermore, this wordsmith developed an amazing feeling for graphic illustrations. The writer Bertolt Brecht once remarked that he loved Luther's works especially because of his 'gestural language'. What he meant was that often the Wittenberg professor's turns of speech make us feel as if we could actually see the gestures that accompany them. For example, in Luther's translation of the Bible, when he writes, *Wenn dein Auge dich ärgert, dann reiß es aus und wirf es weg* (*If your eye annoys you, rip it out and throw it away*).

One of the biggest strengths of Luther's writings, furthermore, is that for all their scholarliness and accuracy they always strove to be understandable. What good would it have done to publish the most erudite specialist literature that only a small minority gets? That's why what the Reformer once said very pointedly about his sermons is equally true for his theological writings: *When I come to the pulpit, it is my intent to preach only to the farmhands and maidservants. I would never stand up for Doctor Jonas' or Melanchthon's[1] sake, not even once. They can read it for themselves in the scriptures.*

In short, from the very start, this clever writer had a large audience in mind, and that is why he succeeded to write in a language that reached the many.

---

[1] Professors Justus Jonas and Philipp Melanchthon were Luther's fellow campaigners in Wittenberg.

From an early time, people urged Luther to publish an edition of his complete works. Rather reluctantly he complied: first his writings in German (1539), later he added the ones he had written in Latin (1545). But he declared, *I thank God that I have heard and found my God in the German language.*

We can see clearly in the prefaces he penned for these editions that the eloquent theologian was not entirely uncritical of his own writings. *My writings*, he announced brightly, *are a shapeless, unstructured mess that even I find hard to sort.* He even apologized for the uneven quality of his work: *Dear reader, when you will now be reading my scribblings, please remember that I was one of those who made progress in writing, not one of those who suddenly go from being nothing at all to being the greatest.*

Does Luther indulge in self-effacing understatement? It might seem so, for he frankly says, *I would have preferred that all my books would have remained in the background and vanished.* At the same time, he blithely declares, *There is hope that, once the current curiosity has run its course, my books won't last for long either.*

Well, in this he could not have been more wrong. His writings are considered to be works of genius. Even today. And they are. But there is a simple explanation for his modest demeanour: Luther saw his books as nothing more than signposts. They were meant to do one thing first and foremost: to give people an appetite for discovering anew the real book, the true 'book of books' – the Bible – for themselves as the source of their 'happiness in life'.

Compared with 'Holy Scripture', all other writings are, from the Reformers' point of view, only insignificant worldly concoctions. Well, maybe Luther didn't even realize how difficult an art it is to make the Bible even accessible (again) to others. He succeeded in doing that. How? That is another thing we will learn from the twelve key texts of the Reformation we will explore in this little book.

LUTHER AND THE REFORMATION

Johann Wolfgang von Goethe once pointedly wrote about the Reformation: 'Just between us, nothing about the whole thing is interesting except Luther's character. Everything else is a muddled rubbish that still bothers us every day.'

Well, this 'muddled rubbish' still has shaken up half the world and made it possible for billions of people to regard God and the world from a new, liberated perspective. Nevertheless, this prince among poets who deemed himself so enlightened consistently pointed out that the great themes and concerns of the Reformation come into laser-sharp focus in the extraordinary character of Martin Luther. To properly engage with Luther's writings, therefore, we must take a quick look at his biography. And I would claim that anyone who is familiar with the man Martin Luther will recognize how often his character proves to be the key to understanding his works.

Instead of offering a historical overview of the Reformation, let me start by taking you into the adventurous existence of a man who 'went forth to unlearn what fear was', condensed into six formative events in

Luther's life that are exemplary for his inner battles, six outstanding experiences that have become part of Reformation history themselves.

Quite possibly, you already know these stories. If you do, no matter. Their density and clarity is such that they are always worth hearing and reading them again. At least I think so.

A PLEDGE IN THE STORM

On July 2, 1505, Martin Luther, a law student of twenty-one years, is caught in a terrible thunderstorm near the village of Stotternheim (north of Erfurt). The storm rages so violently, and lightning strikes so close to the young man, that he is sure he must die. In his unspeakable fear, a question bursts open within him again that has been bothering him for a long time: 'Will I get to heaven?'

Living in fear of the devil since his childhood and regularly punished harshly by his father because of his supposed weaknesses, Luther is convinced that the answer is 'No way'. In his distress, he calls upon St. Anne, the mother of Mary and patron saint of miners who was highly revered at that time and place, and makes this pledge to her: 'Help me, St. Anne! I want to become a monk.' In other words: 'If I survive this, I will enter a monastery.'

Besides his fear of not being good enough for God, Luther has to battle intensely with his family. For his father takes it for granted that his son will become a jurist and enter the family mining business – and that he will obediently marry the bride his parents have chosen for him and sire a horde of children with her. Martin's path in life seems predetermined.

Thus, this pledge becomes a turning point in the young student's life on several levels at once. He survives the thunderstorm, keeps his promise and enters the Augustinian monastery in Erfurt. There, he is free from the clutches of his dominant father, hoping at the same time that among the pious brethren he will be able to live a life that will make him 'worthy' of heaven. At least, the good people of Stotternheim have raised a memorial stone at the site of Luther's 'conversion' and called it 'Turning Point of the Reformation'.

THE TOWER EXPERIENCE

Several years later, possibly in 1515, Martin Luther is sitting in his small study in Wittenberg – after an incredible career within his order. Not only did he become an ordained priest in the monastery, but in the meantime, he also has studied theology, written a dissertation and become a professor at the newly founded university at Wittenberg.

But the question that had brought him into the monastery in the first place is still without an answer: 'What do I have to do to get a merciful God?' Or, in modern terms: What kind of behaviour will give me a guarantee of heaven? He did try everything that a monk's life entails: humbling and chastising himself, going to confession so frequently that his father confessor grew impatient with him, calling on his 14 patron saints twice daily and even going on a pilgrimage to Rome in hopes to finally find peace for his soul. But the uncertainty remained: 'Who can tell me whether I am really saved?'

And then, lightning strikes a second time. This time it comes in the shape of a Bible verse that turns Luther's entire way of thinking upside down. Possibly while preparing a lecture on the Epistle to the Romans, Luther stumbles upon the short but glorious statement, 'The righteous will live by faith'. Reading these words, it suddenly dawns on him – it isn't about what a man or woman *does* at all. You cannot earn God's love and affection, they are freely given – by grace alone. It is enough that a man or woman *believes* in this grace of God.

As Luther himself later described this experience: *In that moment, I felt altogether as if newly born – and I stepped through the open gate into Paradise.*

THE 95 THESES

Three years later, Luther decides it is time to present his liberating insights to the wider public. To this end, he formulates, among other things, '95 Theses on Indulgences'. A popular version of the story is that on October 31, 1517, the evening before All Saints' Day, the professor ostentatiously nailed these theses to the door of the of All Saints' Church in Wittenberg as a call to a scholarly 'disputation'. Whether it really happened like that is still a matter of lively debate. What is certain, though, is that he sent out his theses on that day to several high-ranking church dignitaries.

This is why to this day, October 31, 1517, is considered the hour the Reformation was truly born. Since 1667, October 31 has been observed as Reformation Day each year, because that was the day one individual's insight came to be a topic for everyone.

But Luther, of course, was a child of his time and therefore picked up many of the moods and trends already floating about. One of these was a growing disgust at the selling of indulgences, as it was called. A preacher named Johann Tetzel, for example, roamed the land as the pope's representative with a large entourage and a dazzling stage performance, selling documents that promised their buyers some mitigation of their purgatorial punishments. People were even deluded into thinking they might thus pay the ransom for all their sins and even those of their deceased forebears.

Now this was just the opposite of what Luther thought he had found: for if a human being is justified by faith alone, then these letters of indulgence weren't needed at all. Besides, anyone with a little bit of education knew that the only reason the selling of indulgences was pushed was that the pope had to pay for the construction of the new St. Peter's Basilica and Archbishop Albrecht of Mainz wanted the proceeds to redeem his debt to the Fugger family.

THE DIET OF WORMS

In April 1521, Martin Luther is summoned to Worms, where the Emperor, 30 bishops and countless princes have gathered for the Diet. For those theses did not just make the critical thinker famous, they also made him a rebel who was attacked from all sides.

The pope, for example, has sent a papal bull threatening him with excommunication soon after the theses appeared. It was a warning and a call to back down. Otherwise he would be excluded from the community of the Church. Well, Luther has publicly burned this document, which resulted in him being in fact thrown out of the Roman church. This act was tantamount to a sort of capital punishment at the time.

And now, the newly crowned Emperor Charles wants to examine on the political level what is behind the impetuous scholar. Although 'examine' isn't quite the right word. While Luther is hoping to be allowed to defend and explain his ideas in front of the gathered dignitaries, the princes are interested in one thing only: a revocation. The troublemaker is expected to distance himself from his trouble-stirring works. What's especially annoying to his opponents is that during his journey and at Worms itself, Luther is being celebrated like a popular hero.

After asking for some time to think it over a bit uncertainly on April 17, he is full of confidence on April 18 as he steps in front of the authorities and explains that he is quite willing to let himself be convinced by sound biblical evidence, but feels committed, first and foremost, to God and his conscience – which is why he cannot revoke.

This upright attitude of an individual appealing to the freedom of thought and his own conscience is considered a pivotal moment in the birth of freedom and responsibility for every human being – regardless of status.

THE SOJOURN ON THE WARTBURG

One thing quickly becomes clear in Worms: The Emperor may have promised safe conduct for Luther, but as the Church critic Jan Hus had experienced first-hand a hundred years before, such promises can be brittle. Even with several of the princes on his side, Luther is in danger of ending on a pyre. Especially as the Emperor is starting to hint that he intends to outlaw him shortly. So, a hiding place must be found, and quickly. Luther's prince elector Frederick the Wise comes up with a bright idea – he orchestrates an attack on Luther on the journey home. Riders in masks suddenly break out of the thick forest behind Möhra, brutally drag Luther out of his coach and take him away. The ruse works. Even painter Albrecht Dürer is fully convinced that Luther is dead. All kinds of rumours spread throughout the land. But no one knows anything for sure.

The truth is that Luther is brought to the Wartburg. There, the former monk is given a new identity: a hunting outfit, a sword, a flowing beard, long hair and a few pounds more weight – meet 'Junker Jörg', who from now on lives incognito in a chamber as guest of the lord of the castle.

But while Martin has to live in hiding, several groups insist that after the pious words it is time now for deeds to follow. Some of his adherents – Andreas Karlstadt, for example – proceed to throw all the paintings out of the churches. Luther wants nothing to do with such over the top and violently destructive demonstrations of the Reformers' justified criticism of the veneration of the saints. Others, such as the Zwickau Prophets led by Thomas Müntzer, claim to be receiving messages from God that go far beyond Luther's plans for change and say the time for revolution has come.

Before returning to Wittenberg in order to set things straight again, he translates the New Testament into German within a few weeks. His most precious legacy!

THE WEDDING

On June 13, 1525, Martin Luther marries Katharina von Bora, a nun who – probably with some help from him – escaped from her monastery. This is a very significant step for him, for previously the Reformer merely reacted to many historical developments. Now he sets a trend himself.

Another former monk has already married in 1521, but for a long time, Luther is afraid it could be a danger to the Reformation if he himself got married. His adversaries, after all, are only waiting for that opportunity to triumphantly proclaim he created the movement just to get his bed warmed by a woman (an opportunity they promptly seize when it comes). Furthermore, there was a superstition making the rounds which said that the Anti-Christ would be the offspring of a nun and a monk. As many people were expecting the imminent end of the world anyway, this was a more than disturbing idea.

But there is a prelude to his relationship with Katharina. Luther's constant worrying and his hesitation that followed from it were so great that another woman the Reformer fell in love with soon had enough of it. Ave von Schönfeldt, another former nun, gave up waiting for his proposal and married Basilius Axt in 1524. He was manager of Lucas Cranach's pharmacy.

Katharina von Bora had a similar fate. She too was in love with another man for a long time: Hieronymus Baumgartner, a patrician's son from Nuremberg. But his parents did not give their assent to their son's marriage with an escaped nun.

Thus, the two broken hearts found and comforted each other. Until they decided, in best soap opera fashion, to give it a try together. Luther himself admits that it wasn't the love of their lives in the beginning. But Katharina, sensible, spirited and resourceful, not only got her Martin going again, but the slightly faltering Reformation as well.

This was a quick tour of six stations in Martin Luther's life, landmark experiences that left their marks all over the Reformation writings – above all in the Reformer's passionate desire not only to theologically communicate the secret of the grace of God to the people, but also increasingly to give practical suggestions on how a human life that is assured of this grace of God might look like.

Luther's personal experiences, coupled with his sense of mission, finally led – in conjunction with many other reformatory forces and individuals all over Europe – to the emergence of the 'Protestant Church' in its many forms. The direction the Reformers took was just too opposed to that in which the 'Roman Church' persisted.

At the same time, by radically calling into question traditional structures, institutions and ways of understanding truth, the Reformation laid the foundation for a free society.

THE TWELVE MOST IMPORTANT WORKS

Of course, it is quite brazen for me to claim that I knew which are *the* twelve 'most important' among Martin Luther's writings. So before turning to his works proper, I would like to explain briefly the criteria I have used to select them – and admit right from the start that this list is entirely subjective. So what!

As the purpose of this little book is to introduce you to the essential ideas and thoughts of the Reformation, I have tried to present those texts that have pointed the way forward at critical crossroads. These include, in my opinion, the '95 Theses', as they mark the birth of the Reformation – and thus provide the occasion for the 500th anniversary we celebrate in 2017 – as well as Luther's speech at the Diet of Worms – a defining moment in the history of mankind. These two texts serve as the bookends of my selection.

In a second step, I have included four writings that are considered to be 'main works' of the Reformation because they were highly influential for the course of the Reformation and contain the clearest expressions of Luther's ideas for renewal. These are – according to the unanimous verdict of all scholars – 'On the Freedom of a

Christian', 'On the Babylonian Captivity of the Church', 'To the Christian Nobility of the German Nation', and 'On Worldly Authority'. As I present to you the powerful messages of these texts, you will sense their enormous potential for change.

In the next two works, Luther gives a practical account of the guiding principles of his work. In his 'Open Letter on Translating' he strongly argues why intelligibility is the key to a good Bible translation and explains the guidelines he observed in his own translation. And in his preface to 'The German Mass and Order of Service' he clearly describes what a Christian service should look like if it is to reflect the new theological approaches of the Reformation and to make them palpable.

In a last section, I present to you four writings that show specifically and cleverly that Martin Luther wanted to change society because of his own liberating experiences. In his book, 'On Good Works', he lays the foundation for a Protestant ethic; in 'The Estate of Marriage' he shows the consequences of this new faith for the family; in 'To the Councilmen of All Cities in Germany that they Establish and Maintain Christian Schools' we see the high significance the Reformers placed on education; and in 'Order of a Church Treasure, Advice how to Handle the Spiritual Goods' we find the first traces of Protestant social welfare work. Luther is developing ideas and applications for churches as spiritual communities to take on social and societal responsibilities.

I suppose there are indeed alternative texts that could have gone into this practical section. I think, though, that these will give you a good overview that will help you to easily access further texts.

By the way, in presenting these works I will adhere to a clear pattern. First I give you an 'introduction' with some information on the genesis of each text. Then I provide a comprehensive summary, quoting Luther's key sentences verbatim to make you familiar with each work. And now, let us begin!

THE 95 THESES

With his legendary '95 Theses', Luther became an overnight star. He himself noted later: 'My theses seemed to run through all of Germany within a fortnight.' At least, that was true of the intellectual elite. But it did not take much longer for the common people to realise that something big was going on here.

Yet it was not that uncommon at all for a committed professor to invite other scholars to a public disputation or debate. If there was anything extraordinary about Luther's theses, it was their generous number and the fact that he asked the recipients for written responses. But then the discussions started – so intensely that the envisaged disputation probably never took place.

But let us take a closer look. On October 31, 1507, Luther sent letters with his theses attached to bishops Albrecht von Mainz and Hieronymus Schultz of Brandenburg. Some scholars express doubts as to whether he in fact nailed them to the door of All Saints' Church in Wittenberg on that day. Luther himself does not mention anything of the sort – and the documents in which it is reported (a text by Philipp Melanchthon, for example) were written much later.

Which does not necessarily mean that the whole thing never happened.

The original theses, of which unfortunately no original manuscripts remain, were written in Latin, the language of scholars, and rather grandly titled 'Disputatio pro declaratione virtutis indulgentiarum' (Disputation to discover the efficacy of indulgences). This makes Luther's intention plain: he wanted to find out what indulgences can actually do and whether they had not been massively abused in practice lately.

It is important to realise that at this point, the future Reformer was still convinced of principle that indulgences made sense. He still did not doubt that a person could benefit from the goodness of Saints to balance out his own badness. However, the indulgence preachers were promising relief for 'limbo', as it was called, a sort of 'pre-hell' in which, it was thought, everyone had to await the verdict whether they were destined to go to heaven or hell. Their famous motto was, 'Sobald das Geld im Kasten klingt, die Seele aus dem Feuer springt' (As soon as a coin in the coffer rings, the soul from purgatory springs).

Luther was bothered mainly by the fact that people thought they could simply ransom themselves from their sins with money, that the selling of indulgences had proved a commercial rather than spiritual endeavour and that people were more afraid of purgatory than of hell itself. Thus, he addressed the two bishops, who both were deeply involved in the selling of indulgences, because he could not believe that the pope approved of this undesirable trend: 'I thought I had the pope for my patron, whose trustworthiness I fully relied on at the time.' His trust was soon to be shaken.

Shortly after these letters were sent, some friends of Luther's translated the theses into German and published them without his knowledge, thus ensuring that they indeed became the subject of a public discussion. Now there was no turning back anymore.

The significance the theses had for the Reformer himself, by the way, is evident in the fact that they were the first document he ever signed with his 'new' name. For his original name was 'Luder', but now he found 'Luther', derived from the Greek word 'eleuterios', liberated one, much more fitting.

....

Out of love for the truth and the desire to bring it to light, the following propositions will be discussed at Wittenberg, under the presidency of the Reverend Father Martin Luther, Master of Arts and of Sacred Theology, and Lecturer in Ordinary on the same at that place. ... In the Name of our Lord Jesus Christ. Amen.

After this brisk introduction, the Reformer immediately goes on to the first thesis: *1. Our Lord and Master Jesus Christ, when He said* Repent, *willed that the whole life of believers should be repentance.* – Incidentally, this is about the average length of a thesis.

So Luther wants to emphasize that 'repentance' means first and foremost an inner attitude. Consequently, because guilt and repentance belong together, the pope cannot simply exempt people from any purgatory punishments. To start with, the Church laws for the living have nothing to do with what happens after death: *The dying are freed by death from all penalties; they are already dead to canonical rules, and have a right to be released from them.* In other words, purgatory is not within the Church's jurisdiction at all.

Furthermore, the pain of purgatory really stems from a person's realisation that his or her faith and love on earth have been imperfect. From this point of view, while it is true that a soul should endeavour to increase in love, the pope has no influence whatsoever on that anymore.

It must needs be, therefore, that the people are deceived by that high-sounding promise of release from penalty. Luther goes on to emphasize that we don't even know whether souls in purgatory even want to be 'ransomed'. So anyone claiming that you can buy your salvation with letters of indulgence is lying. If anything, people can be exempted from earthly Church penalties imposed by men by virtue of their 'heavenly credit', the so-called 'graces of pardon'.

And then comes perhaps the most important sentence of the text: *Every truly repentant Christian has a right to full remission of penalty and guilt.* Even without a single letter of indulgence. Because repentance alone is what matters. The implication is clear: As long as someone thinks their penalty has been paid off through indulgences, they are not taking repentance seriously at all.

Of course, the pope should not stop preaching on purgatory. But he must make it clear that the important thing is God's forgiveness and *that the pope does not intend the buying of pardons to be compared in any way to works of mercy.*

Indeed, whoever wants to do something for their soul's salvation should act out of love: *He who gives to the poor or lends to the needy does a better work than buying pardons.* For Christian deeds are an indication that a person understands what faith is all about. *Because love grows by works of love.* Buying indulgences, on the other hand, makes Christians think it is not necessary to act in a Christian way. That is why buyers of indulgences must be taught clearly how wrong they are: Indulgences are *altogether harmful if through them Christians lose their fear of God.*

Assuming that the pope is ignorant of these corruptions regarding the selling of indulgences, Luther proclaims that if the Vicar of Christ in Rome knew about these atrocities, *he would rather that St. Peter's church should go to ashes* than that it should be funded with this kind of mischief – or even that he would sell the cathedral to compensate those who have been ripped off by the indulgence preachers.

By now we have made it to thesis number 51, and now Luther takes another very close look at the practice of indulgences itself. This consists in traveling preachers lodging themselves in a town, forbidding all other church services, preaching daily about nothing but the letters of indulgence and swearing they would pawn their own souls for the indulgences. For the Reformer, all this is a disaster.

Furthermore, according to Luther, it is not clear at all what the *treasures of the Church* that the indulgence preachers are merrily distributing in the pope's name at their sales events are. They cannot be earthly treasures, and the often-mentioned merits of Christ and the Saints work without the pope's help – by grace alone. Therefore, what is being offered can only be the spiritual authority of the pope: *the Most Holy Gospel of the glory and grace of God.*

The content of this gospel, though, is that *it makes the first to be last*, while the selling of indulgences deludes people into thinking that *it makes the last to be first.* Therefore, it should be honestly admitted that the practice prevalent in Germany is nothing but wheeling and dealing for ever higher profits – by people who know nothing of *the grace of God and the piety of the Cross.*

From now on, all support must go to those who truly have the spiritual dimension of the idea of indulgences in mind, which is to set men and women free – and those who abuse it must be stopped. At this point, though, Luther is still so sure of the pope's uprightness that he declares him to be determined *to thunder against those who use the pretext of pardons to contrive the injury of holy love and truth.*

For anyone who seriously claims that even someone who violated Mary the Mother of God could ransom himself with an indulgence must be mad. Besides, what matters is not what kinds of sins can be expunged through a papal pardon, but the Gospel. Therefor the whole discussion is detrimental to the Church: *This unbridled preaching of pardons makes it no easy matter, even for learned men, to rescue the reverence due to the pope.*

Luther goes on to explain in a very clever and diplomatic way the kind of questions he is up against now because of the indulgences: Why does the pope not simply absolve the souls without cost? Why do we pray for the dead so often? Why can a villain buy himself redemption? Why is true repentance forgotten? Why does the pope in Rome with his riches not pay for St. Peter's himself, instead of ransacking other people? Does someone who deeply repents need an indulgence? And why does the pope not keep his own laws?

Without the selling of indulgences, these critical questions from believers would be easy to answer. But then one would have to tell people honestly that happiness simply isn't for sale. And thus, they can *be confident of altering into heaven rather through many tribulations, than through the* (imagined) *assurance of peace.*

ON THE FREEDOM
OF A CHRISTIAN

....

For many theologians and historians, Luther's famous treatise on freedom marks a boundary line in the history of ideas between the Middle Ages and modernity, because it ascribes to man an individual freedom which overcomes all earthly hierarchies, as before God, everyone is lord.

The trigger for writing this work, funnily enough, was pope Leo X's bull of June 15, 1520, threatening Luther with excommunication. For at this time many influential people still believed there could be a peaceful resolution of the conflict with the Reformers. In September of that year, for example, several mediators led by Karl von Miltitz, the papal chamberlain, travelled to Wittenberg in order to move the 'frightful instigator' to agree to a diplomatic solution.

During this conversation, Martin Luther actually expressed his willingness to write a conciliatory letter to the pope – and to attach to it a short work explaining his most important ideas. He probably wrote both texts in October and November, each one in a German and a Latin version.

Yet while in the letter Luther still very kindly declared to have nothing personal against Leo X and even to feel a rapport of 'brotherly love' with him, the 'Sermon on the Freedom of a Christian' soon makes clear how far removed the Reformer's thinking was by now from the hierarchies of clerical power and that there were indeed very high obstacles to a mutual understanding.

The treatise on freedom spread like a wildfire. In the first five years alone it saw twenty print runs in German and eight in Latin. And its effect was that 'freedom' became a sort of central pass word in the local churches: 'We want more freedom.' Albeit while Luther used the term in a solely theological sense, some groups understood it much more comprehensively.

In the '12 Articles of the Upper Swabian Peasants' (which came to be used in some other regions as well), for example, many disgruntled people appealed to the Reformatory idea of freedom and demanded of their lords to put an end to serfdom and to give them a right to a say. When Luther distanced himself from these protests that soon turned violent by writing 'Against the Murderous, Thieving Hordes of Peasants', the result was a long-lasting division in the country. During the following Peasants' War around 100,000 people were killed. That is what Luther had been trying to prevent.

Although, or rather because Luther's idea was received not only in a theological, but also in a social and political sense, it fell on open ears, was debated in the taverns from the North Sea to the Mediterranean, and laid the foundation for a new civil order. Which was, of course, not least due to the fact that for all its complexity, it could be reduced to two memorable sentences: 'A Christian is a perfectly free lord of all, subject to none. A Christian is a perfectly dutiful servant of all, subject to everyone.'

....

It is inevitable that many take offence at Christ, who has been set up as a sign and an offence, so that they fall and rise again. For of course the twofold message just quoted is full of explosive force: a Christian is a free lord. Period. And: he gladly and willingly makes himself a subject. In his treatise, Martin Luther explains in thirty argumentative steps why this is not a contradiction. He starts with an important distinction:

First, we must remember in this context that *man has a twofold nature, a spiritual and a bodily*. Let's consider the spiritual nature first. As there is no earthly thing whatsoever that could free the soul, no earthly thing can take away its freedom either: *The soul has nothing in heaven nor on earth wherein it can live, be right, be free and be Christian, but the sacred Gospel.* In other words: The soul needs nothing for its salvation but the word of God, that is the message of Jesus Christ.

The soul of man who realises that all his works are of no value before God and gives himself to his maker with steadfast faith is free of all earthly bonds. Of course, the many commandments are useful anyway as they help us see our mistakes, but all commandments have already been fulfilled in Christ. The greatest thing, therefore, that God hopes to receive from human beings, is that they put all their trust in him. And if they do, something altogether wonderful happens: Faith *unites the soul with Christ as a bride is united with her bridegroom*, so that it partakes of his *unconquerable righteousness*.

The important thing to remember is: Those who have faith are fulfilling the critical first commandment ('I am the Lord your God. You shall have no other Gods before me.') – and so receive the power to fulfil all the other commandments too. But those who fulfil only the others and neglect the first one will do many things right, but they remain not free and dependent on worldly things.

All this shows that *every Christian is by faith so exalted above all things that by spiritual power he is lord of all things, for nothing can do any harm to his salvation*. Through this inner freedom, a believer has not only the power to respond calmly to all challenges from without, but also the dignity of a priest as he is perpetually in contact with God. To summarize: because the salvation of a Christian is not dependent upon external things and works, he becomes lord of all things. In fact, someone who has already found his salvation in faith just cannot be floored by worldly concerns.

That is why Luther also wants to finally get rid of the distinction between clergy and laity. Furthermore, he demands that this redemptive message should much more frequently be preached in such a way that this liberation is actually experienced. *For when Christ is thus heard in a man's heart, it must rejoice to its very core, and in receiving such comfort grow tender so as to love Christ.*

But what of the bodily man? Luther takes him as seriously as the spiritual man. After all, it might otherwise be suspected that a Christian should lie down lazily and do nothing at all anymore. And because each of us is inward and outward man at the same time, the outer is under Jesus' command to be servant to all. *Here the works begin; here a man cannot take his ease; here he must, indeed, take care to discipline his body by fastings, watchings, labours and other reasonable discipline.* Indeed, it is just when someone understands what God has done for him that it becomes *his one occupation to serve God joyful and for naught, in love that is not constrained* – even if that means he has to overcome his inner temptations over and over again.

Here, Luther deliberately emphasizes: yes, we are supposed to do good works. But the negation follows immediately: these good works have nothing to do with our soul's salvation. So if we do them, please let us not do them out of a sense of duty, but freely. In short: true Christians do not do good so God loves them, but because God loves them.

A wonderful example of this, by the way, are Adam and Eve, who in Paradise had no reason at all to earn God's favour but still gladly did something for him by cultivating and preserving the Garden of Eden. And as all human beings are entering Paradise through faith, as it were, they too are commissioned to take care of the world.

49

But careful, as the Reformer emphasizes once more: *Good works do not make a good man, but a good man does good works.* To put it simply, it works as with a tree: if the tree is healthy, it brings forth good fruit.

Because that is so, there should not be so much talk in Church about what a person should do or not do. What matters is to *look to the person, and to the manner in which it may be justified.* For once someone has experienced the love of God, they also finally have the freedom to stop thinking about themselves all the time, *having nothing before his eyes but the necessities and the advantage of his neighbour. That is the true Christian life, and thus faith goes to work with joy and love, as Paul teaches the Galatians.*

Consequently, the second half of the principal statement follows: *A Christian, being altogether free, should now on the other hand readily make himself a servant to serve, help and in every way act towards his neighbour as he sees that God through Christ has acted and is acting towards him.* Luther goes on to cite several biblical examples of people who were not above doing good for the sake of their neighbour. This, says the Reformer, should also be the understanding that clergy, monasteries and convents have of their work: a pure service to their neighbour, not something which they hope will provide them heavenly benefits: *I will fast, I will pray, I will do this or that, which is commanded me by men, not as having any need of these things for justification or salvation, but that I may thus comply with the will of the pope, of the bishop, of such a community or such a magistrate, or of my neighbour as an exam-*

ple to him; for this cause I will do and suffer all things, just as Christ did and suffered much more for me.

As long as certain works are being done in Christendom because people (egoistically) hope to gain salvation through them, they have not understood what Christian freedom really means. But once believers realise that their works are a consequence of the grace they have experienced, love becomes real.

We conclude therefore that a Christian man does not live in himself, but in Christ, and in his neighbour, or else is no Christian; in Christ by faith, in his neighbour by love. ... This, as you see, is a true and spiritual liberty, making our hearts free from all sins, laws, and commandments; and one which surpasses every other outward liberty, as far as heaven is above earth.

ON THE BABYLONIAN CAPTIVITY OF THE CHURCH

Luther's '95 Theses' have been an invitation to a lively discussion. Which he gets – probably quicker than he bargained for. While the pope is threatening to throw him out of the Church right away, many theologians are busy tackling his ideas for a radical renewal. For example, in June 1520 Augustin von Alveldt publishes a pamphlet in Leipzig in which he harshly condemns the Reformation's approval of offering the chalice to the laity during communion – an idea Luther adopted from early Reformer Jan Hus.

A little later, an Italian Dominican friar named Isidor Isolano writes another treatise in which he resolutely opposes Luther's teachings, which prompts the latter to once again formulate a clear response to his critics. And as his intended audience consists mainly of colleagues and fellow intellectuals, he composes his detailed reply in Latin: 'De captivitate Babylonica ecclesiae praeludium' (= 'On the Babylonian Captivity of the Church').

This work, published in 1520, is one of the foundational texts of the Reformation as it shows Luther clearly parting with several hitherto indispensable ideas of the

Catholic Church, thus pushing ever more unambiguously towards breaking the ties with the Curia. At this point, even the last of all involved realise that Luther's original desire, which was not to found a new Church of his own, but to change the existing Church and make it correspond to its biblical model again, probably won't be fulfilled. That it cannot possibly be fulfilled, as the Reformer is shaking the very foundations of the existing Church.

He does that, among other things, by calling the concept of sacraments into question – in other words, which acts of the Church can be considered sacred and which can not. This distinction remains to this day one of the great challenges for the ecumenical movement. Thus, a wedding is seen as a sacrament in Catholicism, but not in Protestantism. Therefore, even in the 21st century a mixed-denomination couple must decide whether they want to see their church wedding a sacrament or not. If they affirm that, the consequence is that from a Catholic perspective, this marriage cannot be divorced – and all those who are divorced anyway are excluded from the Eucharist.

With his treatise 'On the Babylonian Captivity of the Church', Luther opened the way for these discussions which have been going on for 500 years now. And of course, the term 'captivity' once more conjures up the image of freedom. For in the Reformer's eyes, the Catholic Church is in the terrible situation that within it, many liberating experiences are impossible because it has put itself in chains.

Luther sticks consistently to this imagery and not only graphically explains which kinds of 'captivity' he finds in the practices of the Church, but also expresses his conviction that all believers have become captives. He even goes so far to say that in this kind of Church, even Jesus Christ is a hostage who must be freed as quickly as possible.

Which Luther promptly proceeds to do – as eloquently and vehemently as ever.

....

Right from the start, Luther doesn't mince words: *INDULGENCES ARE A KNAISH TRICK OF THE ROMAN SYCOPHANTS.* Yes, it's all caps even in the original. And then the Reformer makes clear that he came to realise only through the Catholic response to his criticisms that *the papacy is the kingdom of Babylon* – a ruling power, in other words, that is corrupt to the bone.

One senses Luther's disappointment at the aggressive responses of his opponents, whose – in his estimation – inept arguments he quickly dissects, only to declare afterwards that even that is too much attention for them. For his focus in this work is on something much more fundamental – the sacraments, the efficacious signs of God's grace.

At the outset I must deny that there are seven sacraments, and hold for the present to but three – baptism, penance and the bread. These three have been subjected to a miserable captivity by the Roman curia, and the Church has been deprived of all her liberty. From there, Luther goes on to explain in detail what constitutes the captivity of the three sacred acts he still accepts and why he does not want to condone the others at all anymore.

The ongoing dispute about the sacraments was triggered by the question whether laypeople should be allowed to receive the chalice at communion – which was not the custom at the time. This where the Reformer steps in and declares that Jesus's command, 'Drink of it, all of you' cannot mean anything but that every person is invited to drink of the wine. And anyone who should claim that the disciples were all priests is ignorant.

Moreover, the papacy took the position that the entire sacrament was contained in the bread. *If they concede the grace, which is the greater, why not the sign, which is the lesser?* Besides, there are sources that say that the chalice for laypeople used to be entirely accepted in former times. *I conclude, then, that it is wicked and despotic to deny both kinds to the laity.* The most tragic thing for Luther lies in the fact that this dispute reveals a threefold 'captivity'.

- The first captivity: The papacy has taken the right to a complete Lord's Supper away from the people.
- The second captivity: The papacy claims that in *transubstantiation – forsooth, a monstrous word for a monstrous idea! –*, the bread is miraculously turned into flesh. Luther is convinced that this is a meaningless attempt to explain something that needs no explanation: *Why should not Christ include His body in the*

substance of the bread ...? When Jesus says, 'This bread is my body', he does not need any magic tricks.

- The third captivity: Through all this big fuss, the papacy is making people believe that the Lord's Supper is a 'sacrifice'. But that is a complete misunderstanding. Neither the Lord's supper nor the Mass are about man having to offer something but about man being given a promise. But *if the Mass is a promise, ... it is to be approached, not with any work or strength or merit, but with faith alone.* This is a fundamental criticism of the way the Catholic Church views the service. To put it another way: For Luther, it is obvious that in the service, God serves man, not the other way around. That is why he finds it intolerable that faith *in the word from which all good things flow* is being obliterated by an abundance of ritual: *For when faith dies ..., works and the traditions of works immediately crowd into their place.*

All these 'captivities' had the effect of making an individual's personal faith less and less important. Luther goes on to ask himself this heretical question: *Will you not overturn the practice and teaching of all the churches and monasteries? ... I answer: This is the very thing ...* The actions of Jesus, who at the Lord's Supper simply sat down to eat with his disciples and passed them the bread and the wine without much ado, shall become the model for our services again.

After these fundamental considerations, Luther now turns to the sacrament of baptism, which he thinks is being harassed *by the filthy and godless monsters of greed and superstition.* His focus here is not so much on the act of baptism itself as on emphasizing the permanent nature of baptism. If through baptism, man belongs unchangeably to God, the papacy cannot keep declaring that the salvation of believers is in jeopardy: *Even if* (a Christian) *would, he cannot lose his salvation, however much he sins, unless he will not believe.*

Again, the emphasis is on faith, the most important thing of all! Constant talk about man's sins just distracts from the centre. This is why we could also say, that it is always about the *sacraments of justifying faith and not of works. Their whole efficacy, therefore, consists in faith itself, not in the doing of a work.* Consequently: *Who gave him* (the pope) *power to despoil us of this liberty, granted us in baptism?*

While he is on a roll, Luther goes on to demand the abolition of all vows, which also create the impression that a performance is needed to earn God's goodwill. For him this includes, of course, the monastic vows.

The third sacrament tackled by Luther is penance. *The promise of penance* has turned into *the most oppressive despotism of all and serves to establish a more than temporal rule.* In a nutshell: *A contrite heart is a precious thing, but it is found only where there is a lively faith in the promises and the threats of God.* Therefore, none should think they could achieve salvation by penitentiary exercises of any kind. For penance, after all, is not a performance but a lifelong attitude.

Confession as such, according to the Reformer, makes a lot of sense. *This alone do I abominate, – that this confession has been subjected to the despotism and extortion of the pontiffs.* Pilgrimages, veneration of Saints, spiritual exercises and many other things are there to make people believe they could do something for their own salvation.

Finally, Luther explains why the other sacraments of the Catholic Church aren't really sacraments at all: because they are not mentioned in Scripture as signs of God's grace – neither confirmation (which is not mentioned at all) nor ordination (because before God, all believers are priests) nor the last rites (as prayers for the sick are built on the hope that they may be healed) nor marriage (which is equally present in non-Christian cultures.)

From that point of view, the Reformer also argues for an abolition of the Catholic rules of marriage. Indeed, although he rejects divorce, he holds that the Bible allows it. And as not even penance is introduced by Jesus as a special sacred act, Luther ends with this insight: *Hence there are, strictly speaking, but two sacraments in the Church of God – baptism and bread; for only in these two do we find both the divinely instituted sign and the promise of forgiveness of sins.*

TO THE CHRISTIAN NOBILITY
OF THE GERMAN NATION

The so-called 'nobility tract' made Martin Luther a popular hero. If hitherto there had 'only' been a rebellious
monk ranting about some disagreements within the
Church, it now became unmistakably clear that much
more than that was at stake. This was about a great religious – and consequently political – process of renewal.
This was about us!

At the same time, the Reformation tract 'To the
Christian Nobility of the German Nation' showed like
few other what a great strategist the professor from
Wittenberg was. For Luther needed allies. He had realised by now that disputations and debates, even among
the greatest minds, were not enough to change Christianity. The Reformation needed fellow campaigners
outside the Church.

With that in mind, in 1520 the spiritual revolutionary boldly addressed the whole range of secular powers.
To paraphrase his message to the rulers: 'We Germans
are being ripped off by the pope. We must stick together
lest the clerical powers in Rome put us down. Let us

change the Church and the world together – our deca-
dent bishops obviously cannot do it.'

There is a very impressive theological sleight of hand
behind this, by the way. Luther shows that the Roman
claim that only priests should be allowed to interpret
the Bible does not hold water. Every Christian has the
right to spiritual action and involvement in shaping
the Church. In this context, the important expression
'priesthood of all believers' turns up for the first time,
which of course implies: You rulers of the countries
have the same right to renew the Church as the pope.
So let's do it!

And Luther's strategy paid off. Without the support
of the nobility, the Reformatory endeavour would have
had no chance of success. Just the fact that Frederick
the Wise, Elector of Saxony and thus Luther's sovereign,
was supporting the movement made sure that neither
Luther's excommunication nor his outlawry could really
be executed. Luther merrily continued to lead services,
and no one arrested him.

Of course, behind the manifold support that the Reformation received from the 'Christian nobility of the
German nation', there were not only serious spiritual
convictions. A diversity of power interests played a role
too. At a time when cities flowered and horizons ex-
panded – just think of the discovery of America only
30 years before or of the writings of Nicolaus Coper-
nicus that were turning the image of the world upside
down by claiming that the Earth is not the centre of the
universe – the princes were trying to find a new role

for themselves and take a bold stand against Emperor and pope.

We might truthfully say, therefore, that Martin Luther was in the right time and place when he started pushing for renewal. Social change was in the air. And because of that, the 'nobility tract' turned out to be a huge success. Dozens of pirate editions made sure it spread quickly. And Frederick the Wise sent Luther a substantial roast of venison to thank him for it.

....

To His Most Illustrious and Mighty Imperial Majesty, and to the Christian Nobility of the German Nation, Doctor Martin Luther. The tone is dignified and formal. And the Reformer chooses a clever opening by saying: I speak on behalf of the many discontented in the land, asking myself whether *God may inspire someone with His Spirit to land this suffering nation a helping hand.* (By 'suffering', Luther means poor and bled dry by the Roman Church.)

The important thing, of course, is to build this renewal first and foremost on the power of God. But that is just the argument hitherto used by the papacy to keep the secular princes down. *Let us act wisely, therefore, and in God's fear.*

For the Roman clergy has cleverly built three 'walls' around itself, *in such wise that no one has been able to reform them; and this has been the cause of terrible corruption throughout all Christendom.*

The papacy always claims that spiritual power is higher than secular power.

The papacy always claims that the pope alone knows how to interpret the Bible correctly.

The papacy declares categorically that only the pope can call a council.

And they have intimidated kings and princes by making them believe it would be an offence against God not to obey them in all these knavish, crafty deceptions.

Now Luther wants to *blow down these walls* of the papacy, just as the walls of Jericho were overthrown with trumpets.

And he promptly directs his first attack against the first wall. For the fundamental problem lies, in his view, in the *invention* of a separation between the spiritual and the temporal estate. Why? Simply because *all Christians are truly of the 'spiritual estate'*. In other words, all Christians, having the same baptism, the same gospel and the same faith, are 'spiritual people' and thus priests. To underpin that, Luther cites, among others, a verse from the Book of Revelation: 'And hast made us unto our God kings and priests.' This ordination is more important than all Church ordinations.

Although individuals are chosen from this group of all priests to be invested with certain offices, this has nothing to do with any special estate. Indeed, if a group of Christians in the wilderness would choose one from their midst, this person *would be as truly a priest as though all bishops and popes had consecrated him*. In this sense, of course, all secular rulers, in other words the addressees of this tract, are priests too. *For whoever comes out of the water of baptism can boast that he is already consecrated priest, bishop and pope, though it is not seemly that everyone should exercise the office.*

What Luther demands here, then, is a democratization of the Church. The community should decide who will receive a clerical office and who will not – and from whom it will be taken. *Beyond all doubt, then, a priest is no longer a priest when he is deposed.* The papacy, though, acts as if there were a 'sacred' estate of spiritual offices. But the truth is, whether pope, prince, shoemaker or peasant – *they are all alike consecrated priests and bishops.*

But if all are members of the body of Christ in the same way, of course the secular authorities have the right to harry or punish the spiritual authorities. It even is their duty. *All that the canon law has said to the contrary is sheer invention of Roman presumption.* It certainly was not a good spirit that wanted to put the clergy above the temporal law and the Christian community. For *every man shall esteem himself the lowliest and the least.*

This brings Luther to the second wall, which he thinks is *still more flimsy and worthless.* The idea that the pope and the curia are *the only Masters of the Holy Scriptures* is, after all, absolutely bizarre, not to mention the great number of heretical and godless canon laws that have proven it wrong again and again. The curia may claim to have the Holy Spirit as much as they like, it won't help them.

Luther sees his view confirmed even in the Bible itself: 'If a revelation is made to another sitting there, let the first be silent' (1 Cor. 14:30). Evidently there were spiritual disputes even in the earliest Christian community. Besides, how do we know that the sitting pope is even a real Christian at all?

Of course, the head of the Church likes to point out that Jesus gave the 'key' to Peter. But Luther argues, firstly, that this refers to the Church as a whole, and secondly, the context is that the disciple is given authority to bind to or release from sin. Not one word here refers to any exclusive authority to interpret the Bible.

Furthermore, Jesus prayed for *all Apostles and Christians, as he says in John 17: 'Father, I pray for those whom Thou hast given Me, and not for these only, but for all who believe on Me through their word.'* Clearly, even beyond the immediate circle of those called by Jesus, people can have the right Spirit.

But if it is true that all are 'priests', then why *should not we perceive what squares with faith and what does not, as well as does an unbelieving pope?* Thus, the papacy may and should be forced to *follow not their own interpretation, but the one that is better. ... Therefore it behooves every Christian to espouse the cause of the faith, to understand and defend it, and to rebuke all errors.*

Having cleared away these first two nasty walls, the third one falls of itself. Why? Simple. As each member of the body of Christ is called to take care of the others, each of them also has the right to call a council. The pope's presumption that only he has that right is therefore entirely unbiblical. Incidentally, even the Council of Jerusalem – the first council of all – was not called by Peter, but by the early Christian community. And the famous Council of Nicaea was gathered by the Emperor

Constantine. Therefore, even today the temporal power has the right to organize a council.

Luther goes on to appeal to the princes in no uncertain terms to do their duty and call such a clerical assembly, which would then have the authority to make changes in the Church happen. *Therefore, if the pope were to use his authority to prevent the calling of a free council, and thus became a hindrance to the edification of the Church, we should have regard neither for him nor for his authority ... It is only the power of the devil ... which resists the things that serve for the edification of Christendom.*

Yes, even if a miraculous sign would occur and create the impression that the pope is right and the temporal power wrong, that sign would certainly be coming from the devil. Consequently, Luther encourages the princes to become fearless Reformers. *Let us, therefore, hold fast to this: No Christian authority can do anything against Christ. ... Thus I hope that the false, lying terror with which the Romans have this long time made our conscience timid and stupid, has been allayed.*

ON WORLDLY AUTHORITY

In the fall of 1522, Luther's translation of the New Testament appeared, the so-called 'September Testament'. It was a huge success – while at the same time triggering massive quarrels. For George the Bearded, the ruler in the other part of Saxony, immediately exercised censorship and forbade the selling of the 'heretical' Bible translation. He even went so far as to issue a decree making it a punishable offence to buy or sell this publication. Anyone who had already purchased a copy had to turn it over for a refund – by Christmas.

So it was not a coincidence that Luther finished his landmark treatise on authority just on Christmas Day 1522, not without giving a sort of dedication to the stubborn Saxon right at the beginning.

But there were two other occasions for the treatise. For one thing, Duke John of Saxony had asked Luther to explain to him how the rule of a prince squared with the Christian faith; for another, the so-called 'Schwärmer' (zealot) movement had taken the 'Freedom of a Christian' in an eminently political way and were radically calling the rule of 'lords' into question.

Consequently, Martin Luther was facing the dilemma of having to provide clarification for several areas of conflict at once: How is 'temporal authority' compatible with 'spiritual freedom'? Does the prince of a country have the right to forbid a Bible translation? Does a Christian have the right to oppose his 'lord's' arbitrary, godless behaviour? And how far does a Christian's freedom go in real life?

That this was more than just academic skirmishes, but a matter of life or death, became decisively clear in 1527, when George the Bearded had a bookseller named Johannes Herrgott executed on Leipzig's market square. At the same time, in writing his treatise Luther had to exercise much diplomatic restraint so as to cause not too much offence to the princes, to whom he had only recently ascribed such a great responsibility for the renewal of the Church.

The central theses in the treatise 'On Worldly Authority: How Far Does the Obedience Owed to It Extend?' later became known as the 'Two kingdoms doctrine'. Luther himself did not use that term, but he made it abundantly clear that in his view, man is living in two overlapping spheres of power – the Kingdom of God and the kingdom of the world. This enabled him to separate the respective jurisdictions in such a way as to offer something approaching a solution for the problems outlined above.

The text is assumed to have been published in early March 1523. At least we know that on March 21, 1523, George the Bearded officially complained to Elector

Frederick the Wise about this work, in which he is not treated very kindly. Frederick remained calm. Maybe he already knew 500 years ago that nothing boosts the sales of a book more than when it is forbidden somewhere. And indeed, both the treatise on authority and Luther's translation of the New Testament proved to be real bestsellers.

....

Some time ago, I wrote a pamphlet to the German nobility. ... How much notice they took of it is plain for all to see. Luther's hopes that all authorities would take his side have been shattered; only some of them follow him. Now he must determine how to deal with princes who *think they can command their subjects whatever they like and do with them as they please. And their subjects are just as deluded, and believe (wrongly) that they must obey them in all things.* But above all, the Reformer wants to address the 'lords' who are presuming to command what people believe. So he *must resist them, even if it is only with words.*

The Reformer begins by explaining in detail why he sees the secular law as being, in principle, ordained by God. At the same time, though, he points to the many Bible verses proving that Jesus overcomes earthly laws. So there seem to be two different levels present here: the Kingdom of God and the kingdom of the world. In the Kingdom of God, to which all true believers belong, Jesus Christ alone rules. That means that if everyone were a true Christian, no secular law would be needed anymore at all. For then everyone would live in such a way as to pursuing the best interests of their neighbour.

Unfortunately, though, there also are unrighteous people. And for them, a secular order is needed. In other words: *Those who ... are not Christians ... belong ... to the kingdom of the world.* Clear rules are needed to curb their iniquity. *And so God has ordained the two governments, the spiritual, which fashions true Christians and just persons through the Holy Spirit under Christ, and the secular government, which holds the Unchristian and wicked in check and forces them to keep the peace.*

As there will never be a purely Christian society, both understandings of law will still be necessary. The most important thing in this context is to clearly define the jurisdiction for each. For Christians in fact are, and will remain, part of secular society – and they recognise temporal authority because they know how important it is for 'unbelievers'.

This implies, for example, that Christians will never take up the sword against each other or for their own purposes, but that it can be necessary to use arms under the secular government – even out of love, if it serves to relieve a neighbour's need. *My dear brother, do not presume to say that the Christian must not do what is in fact God's own work, ordinance and creation.*

Luther's manifold arguments show how contentiously the relationship between Christians and arms was being discussed even then, and they converge in the idea that *Christians are neither to employ nor to call on the sword for themselves and in their own concerns. But they may and should use it and call on it for the sake of others, so that evil may be prevented and justice upheld.* From this perspective, even judges and executioners can be true Christians.

In the second part of his treatise, Martin Luther asks the question how far worldly authority extends and how we can make sure that it does not intrude into the Kingdom of God. *We now come to the main part of this treatise.*

The line drawn by the Reformer is really very clear – the worldly authority is responsible for the outer man and his possessions, the spiritual government takes care of his soul. And whenever worldly rulers think they could meddle with man's soul and salvation, they act against Jesus Christ. For Luther, though, the clerical authority belongs to the secular government too, especially as it keeps ordaining things that are clearly harmful for the souls of men. Within the spiritual government, Christ alone reigns, as no worldly institution can have power over the soul. *Would anyone in his right mind give orders where he has no authority?* In other words, things that concern salvation must be negotiated directly between man and God.

Consequently, while worldly rulers have power over man's body, his thoughts are free. Any prince who seriously thinks he could order the way their subjects think is horribly mistaken. The question which government is responsible in a given situation always must be examined. That is why Jesus himself said: 'Therefore render to Caesar the things that are Caesar's, and to God the things that are God's.'

So, if a prince or secular lord commands you to adhere to the papacy, to believe this or that, or to surrender books, then your answer should be: ... My good Lord, I owe you obedience with my life and goods. Command me what lies within the limits of your authority, and I will obey. But if you command me to believe, or to surrender my books, I will not obey. For then you will have become a tyrant ..., commanding where you have neither right nor power.

And then, Luther gets very specific: The Christians within the principality where his translation of the New Testament has been forbidden should refuse to hand over their copies, precisely because there are, unfortunately, so few princes who are believers. Besides, it is never the princes' responsibility, Luther emphasizes, to resolve spiritual disputes through force; not even by acting forcibly against heretics. Words and arguments alone, says the Reformer, should clear up these matters.

The resolution of such conflicts, by the way, belongs to the jurisdiction of the clerical authorities – mind you, without arms. *As has been said, Christians can be governed by nothing except the Word of God alone.*

This brings Luther to the third part of his work: How should a prince then act? *Now, whoever wants to be a Christian prince must abandon any intention of lording it over people and using force.* In other words, on the one hand a ruler should keep a firm grip on the law, while on the other, he must ask himself in each individual situation whether what he is doing is right. *It is precisely with reference to this that I said that the prince's office is beset by dangers.*

The best way to approach it is for a prince to see himself as a servant to his subjects. *I am not to see how I can lord it over them, but how they may be protected and defended.* To achieve that, it is of course helpful to look to Jesus and act like he did.

To govern in a Christian way, a prince should listen to his counsellors and respect them while keeping a watchful eye on them. *You do have to take the risk of entrusting people with offices, but you must not trust them or rely on them, but on God alone.*

Furthermore, a prince shall be careful not to deal out excessive punishment – not least to avoid harm for himself. *Where an injustice cannot be punished without a greater injustice, he should not insist on his rights, however just his cause.*

Therefore, princes should not start wars, least of all against higher powers, but they should defend the rights of their subjects with arms, if need be. If a ruler is clearly in the wrong, though, a Christian has the right to refuse conscription. For *we must obey God rather than men.*

All this can be achieved when a prince asks God for wisdom – in faith and with heartfelt prayer. For then, even controversial decisions will always be governed by the yardstick of love.

With his teaching of the two 'powers', Luther really is the first to make a clear distinction between state and religion. That is why this treatise is often considered to be a foundational document of Western democracy.

OPEN LETTER ON TRANSLATING

During the summer of 1530, Martin Luther was stuck at Coburg Fortress while at the Diet of Augsburg, Emperor Charles V was debating with the princes of the land how the unit of the Church could be restored. At least the Lutherans were, for the first time, recognized as negotiating partners of equal rank. Except Luther himself. Of course. He was an outlaw, after all, so the Emperor's soldiers would have arrested him on the spot. So the Reformer in his 'exile' was reduced to hearing from his fellow campaigner Philipp Melanchthon about the developments.

And it did not look good. For Johannes Eck, one of the negotiators on the papal side, had prepared '404 Articles' in advance in which he – as he firmly believed – proved the Reformers wrong and heretical in hundreds of cases. Thus, the delegates from Wittenberg, who had been planning to tread very carefully, found themselves faced with the necessity to formulate a confessional creed of their own.

So they wrote, in great haste, the document that was to become famous as 'Confessio Augustana', the

'Augsburg Confession', a sort of foundation programme for the Protestant faith. Even here, the supporters of the Reformation wanted to show, above all, that their teachings as such were not so very different from those of the Roman Church at all; they just distanced themselves from some abuses that had crept in over time.

The papal side immediately set about refuting the 'Confessio', first in a very polemic fashion that was rejected by everyone, then in a more objective discussion. With that, the Emperor saw the views of the Reformers as disproved and gave the Protestants an ultimatum to submit to the Church. But they refused and left the city.

There was one special highlight in all these disputes, though. In Augsburg Martin Luther, who claimed again and again to be deriving all his insights from the Bible, was accused of having distorted Holy Scripture himself.

Yes! For the Greek original of the sentence so often quoted by all Reformers, 'Man is justified by faith alone', does not contain the words 'alone' or 'only' at all. In other words, Luther put it in there to bend the Bible into the shape he preferred. And someone who manipulated the Bible like that could not claim to stand on it.

Naturally, Luther could not stand for that. And as he was reduced to idleness anyway, having to follow the Diet's proceedings from afar, he sat down right away and formulated a rebuttal – the 'Open Letter on Translating'. On the one hand, this was his response to the specific accusation of having manipulated the text when he translated it, but on the other, he took the opportunity to explain to the world the principles which had guided him in his translation of the Bible.

The 'Open Letter', which in its complete form contains a second part about the 'Intercessions of the Saints', shows Luther to be an erudite and linguistically well versed scholar who contributed much to the further development of the German language, not just with his memorable turns of phrase that are still widely in use today, but also with his reflections on how communication can be achieved successfully at all.

....

Grace and peace in Christ, honourable, worthy and dear Lord and friend! After this friendly greeting, Luther gets right into the point – namely, answering the question how to translate the verse 'that one is justified by faith alone apart from works of law'. *And you also tell me that the papists are causing a great fuss because Paul's text does not contain the word* sola *(alone).*

'Well,' Luther comments briskly, instead of griping, the 'enemies of the truth' as he calls them, might have had a go at translating the Bible themselves. Now they are busy using the translation – and at the same time complaining whenever something does not suit them. So the Reformer makes it emphatically clear that he proceeded to the best of his ability – and that everyone is free to create their own, more accurate translation. After all, no one is under any obligation to adopt his text.

Furthermore, Luther points out calmly that even St. Jerome encountered criticism from all those wiseacres who would never have been able to do it themselves: *The world believes itself to be the expert in everything, while putting the bit under the horse's tail. Criticizing everything and accomplishing nothing, that is the world's nature.*

The theologian is especially amused by the fact that someone in Dresden has published his translation under his own name – and reaps applause for it everywhere, just because he is a papist. So the plagiarist is getting all the credit, while Luther's version is officially banned there. But the Reformer takes a very relaxed view on that. After all, this means that even his enemies are encountering the new translation

But back to the question at hand, Luther continues. If such an asinine question must be answered, his own competence should be emphasized first: He is a scholar, a doctor, preacher, theologian, philosopher, dialectician and writer. Even if all that were true of some of his opponents, Luther stresses that beyond all these things, he is also an exegete, a translator and a great man of prayer. *They, too, are well aware that I can do everything they can do. Yet they treat me as a stranger in their discipline.*

Thus, the Reformer recommends answering these donkeys' braying simply by saying *Luther will have it so.* Period. Nevertheless, for his addressee (and for his fellow campaigners) he is willing to explain in short why he has put the word 'alone' in there. And he does that by pointing out his principles in translating:

I have always tried to translate in a pure and clear German. This is so important to Luther that he sometimes spent four weeks to search for the proper word. Not always successfully. Not everyone, however, is able to discern how much care went into the finished product.

To put it more specifically: Naturally, the Reformer knows that Paul has not literally written 'by faith alone' – he didn't need his opponents to point that out to him. It is just that in German, when things are put opposite each other, you say 'not this, but "only" that'. And when the original text suggests such an opposition of concepts, the rules of the target language of your translation should be applied. *To be sure, I can also say, 'The farmer brings grain and* kein *money,' but the words* 'kein *money' do not sound as full and clear as if I were to say, 'the farmer brings* allein *grain and* kein *money*. Only the word 'allein' makes the context unambiguously clear in German.

What follows is one of Luther's most frequently quoted sayings: *We do not have to ask the literal Latin how we are to speak German, as these donkeys do. Rather we must ask the other in the home, the children on the street, the common man in the marketplace. We must look at their mouth to see how they speak, and do our translating accordingly.*

Translating as people are talking with each other every day – that is Luther's ideal. So when the Latin text talks about the 'excessiveness of the heart' (*Tell me, is that speaking German?*), you just write, 'Wes das Herz voll ist, des gehet der Mund über' (What fills the heart overflows the mouth). And when Judas says in the original, 'Why has this loss of ointment occurred?', it would be absurd to write that down word for word in German. Better translate thus – even if it is a paraphrase: 'Why this extravagance? It is a shame about the ointment.' Just as no average German understands the meaning of 'Maria, voll Gnaden' (Mary, full of grace). Reason enough to prefer addressing her as 'du Holdselige' (thou pleasing one) or even simply 'liebe Maria' (dear Mary).

Anyone who knows German also knows what a heart word 'liebe' is: dear Mary, dear God, the dear emperor, the dear prince, the dear man, the dear child. I do not know if one can say this word 'liebe' in Latin or in other languages with so much depth of feeling, so that it goes to the heart and resonates there, through all the senses, as it does in our language.

Words, after all, have their own power in every language. So you have to look very carefully whether a literal translation really transports the original meaning. *A translator must have a large store of words so that he can have them all ready when one word does not fit in every context.*

From that point of view, Luther points out once more that he is not willing to explain his reasoning behind every word in his translation. After all, he has done his job to the best of his ability.

To illustrate how carefully and conscientiously he proceeded, Luther goes on to cite some examples where he did after all give preference to a literal translation in order to preserve the accurate theological meaning, even though he probably could have found beautiful colloquial turns of phrase.

All this goes to show that a great sense of responsibility is essential for this work. *Translating is not everyone's skill as some mad saints imagine. It requires a right, devout, honest, sincere, God-fearing, Christian, trained, edu-*

cated, and experienced heart. So I hold that no false Christian or sectarian spirit can be a good translator.

In other words, Paul's intention in his Epistle to the Romans made it necessary to add 'alone'. If we are not justified by works, then it follows that we are justified by faith *alone*. Besides, the theological focus is on the first part of the verse anyway: 'Man is justified apart from works of the law.' So if anyone wants to get worked up, let them get worked up about this – and not about the little word 'alone' in the second half of the verse. For the real challenge lies in the content, not in the phrasing.

Finally, Luther concludes with a short explanation of his doctrine of justification to make sure that everyone understands why this statement from Romans is so existentially significant. *Now if it is not works, it must be faith alone. ... Therefore, it will remain in my New Testament.*

THE GERMAN MASS AND
ORDER OF SERVICE

....

The more passionately the Reformers grappled with the deplorable developments within the Catholic Church, the clearer it became that all this had to have consequences for the shape of Christian services and so for the Christians' everyday life.

Martin Luther himself hesitated at first, but when more and more of his fellow campaigners (as well as some of his opponents, such as Thomas Müntzer) started to translate parts of the traditional Latin Mass into German, he soon realised he had to speak up on the subject. And speak up he did.

In 1523, Luther started by publishing two short treatises on reforming the service: 'Von der Ordnung des Gottesdienstes in der Gemeinde' (On the Order of Service in the Church) in German and 'Formula missae et communionis' in Latin. Neither of them formulates any specific orders of service yet, though. Instead, they are programmatic sketches to make clear what the necessary corrections are about.

For the Reformer mainly saw three flaws that he wanted to redress: the poor quality of sermons (if indeed there was a sermon at all), the lack of participation by the congregation in the events of the service (partly due to the hitherto practiced exclusion of the congregation from the chalice at Eucharist) and the liturgical understanding of the Sacrifice of the Mass that still made it appear as if a person could earn God's favour.

In 1526, Luther described what such a service held in German might look like in his so-called 'German Mass', where he endeavours to overcome the medieval structure of the service and turn what happens on a Sunday into a real celebration of faith again.

In this order of service, first put to the text in 1525 in Wittenberg, Luther created not just new translations, but new melodies as well for the liturgical singing. At the same time, though, he emphasizes that these formulae are to be seen as preliminary suggestions and by no means as binding.

Amongst many small changes in the elements of the service, Luther's focus was, as mentioned, first and foremost on the principal understanding. While the Catholic Mass was then dominated by the idea that man was doing something for God, this was an unbearable thought for Luther. If man indeed is justified 'by faith alone', then it must be God himself who acts and works in the service.

And that was a real paradigm shift. The question no longer was how man can please God, but how the service expresses the fact that man pleases God. That is why Luther is using the word 'beneficium', gift, again and again with respect to the service. It is man who receives a gift from God in the service. And this gift should be experienced with all senses.

As inspiring as it certainly would be to look closely at the entire 'German Mass', I will here restrict myself to the preface as it summarizes Luther's essential thoughts about the service.

....

Above all things, I ... beseech all, who see or desire to observe this our Order of Divine Service, on no account to make of it a compulsory law, ... but to use it agreeable to Christian liberty at their good pleasure. A strong curtain raiser. Churches are supposed to be inspired by Luther's work, but they remain entirely free to adapt the service to their specific needs.

Still, the Reformer knows some sort of structure must be brought into the proliferation of new liturgies on all sides: *Where, then, it happens that men are offended or perplexed at such diversity of use, we are truly bound to put limits to liberty; and, so far as possible, to endeavour that the people are bettered by what we do and not offended.* Besides, it only makes sense that all Christians be *of like ways and fashion.*

This does not mean that all churches should apply the Wittenberg order, just that within a principality, a certain consistency should be sought. The guiding principle should be that the orders of service must be oriented towards those *who are not yet Christians.* They are *for the simple and for the young folk who must daily be exercised in the Scripture and God's word ... For the sake of such, we must read, sing, preach, write, and compose.* Luther even adds that the evil of papal services consists precisely in this, that they are directed towards and aim to benefit insiders only. *And that is the devil.*

Generally speaking, Luther envisions three different forms of service. First the Latin Mass, which should by no means be abolished. It would even be desirable, if only because of the training in languages involved, to have services in Greek and Hebrew too. *For I would gladly raise up a generation able to be of use to Christ in foreign lands and to talk with their people.* How else would one do justice to the missionary impulse of the traveling apostles?

The second form of service is the German Mass, which is specifically geared towards those who *are not yet believers or Christians.* Such a service is *a public allurement to faith and Christianity* and we must always keep in mind that many people know nothing at all about liturgy, but stand there *just as if we held Divine Service in an open square or field amongst Turks or heathen.*

The third form of service is less public and directed towards those *who are desirous of being Christians in earnest, and are ready to profess the Gospel with hand and mouth.* Such meetings should take place in private homes and, as we would now say, break down the faith into everyday life. *Here there would not be need of much fine singing. Here we could have baptism and the sacrament in short and simple fashion: and direct everything towards the Word and prayer and love.*

Luther himself admits, though, that he does not have the right people for such an intense community. *Nor do I see many who are urgent for it.* Thus, for the time being, he concentrates on the first two forms: a service for insiders and a more missionary service that *shall ... call and excite others to faith.* Services are certainly necessary, *for we Germans are a wild, rude, tempestuous people; with whom one must not lightly make experiment in anything new, unless there be most urgent need.*

So what is needed for the German order of service, for which Luther then goes on to develop very specific elements? Simply that it should be an instruction, an event *by which heathen, desirous of becoming Christians, are taught and shown what they are to believe, to do, to leave undone and to know in Christianity.*

The model for this goes back to the instruction of the catechumens – those who in the early middle ages received an instruction in the faith before being baptized. Their schooling materials consisted mainly of the Ten Commandments, the Creed and the Lord's Prayer. These basics are now to be imparted in the newly developed services and to be deepened at home. What is important is that people do not just memorize the words but really understand what they are about.

They should be questioned like this: ... What does it mean when you say, Our Father in heaven? Answer: That God is not an earthly but a heavenly Father who would make us rich and blessed in heaven. In other words, Luther wants the service to stimulate serious discussion of the faith among the people. In the end, the two most important truths of the Gospel should be brought home to them: *Faith's pouch may have two purses. Into the one we put this, that ... we are all corrupt, sinners and under condemnation. Into the other purse we put this, that we are all saved through Jesus Christ from such corruption sin and condemnation.*

Something similar is true about love. People shall learn that a Christian should do everyone good and can suffer all evil. Once someone understands this essential idea, they can be encouraged to memorize Bible verses. This one from Romans, for example: 'Christ was delivered up for our trespasses and was raised again for our justification.' Or words from Matthew's Gospel such as: 'What ye have done unto one of the least of these my brethren, ye have done unto me.'

If that sounds a little pedagogical, that is exactly what Luther desires: *Let none think himself too wise for this and despise such child's play. Christ, in order to train men, must needs become a man himself. If we wish to train children, we must become children with them.*

Thus, the Reformer does not shy away from elementarising the truths of the faith and communicating them through the most illustrative methods. Behind this is his strong desire to see the substance of the sermon realised in people's lives. And if all sorts of new ideas about communication are needed for that, then why not?

Otherwise things will remain as they have been, a daily going to church and a coming away again. The essential thing is and will always be that the Gospel is reaching the people. For, as Luther summarizes the ideas in his preface, *enough is written in the books, yes; but it has not been driven home to the hearts.*

Luther then goes on to explain in detail the service elements through which he wants to achieve this. But that is a little beyond our scope.

ON GOOD WORKS

'If it goes on like this, it is, in my opinion, going to be the best of all my books,' wrote Martin Luther to Georg Spalatin, secretary and theological counsellor to Elector Frederick, on March 25, 1520. Spalatin had asked the Reformer to put into words what the reformatory insights actually meant for people's conduct.

And so, Luther set to work. Between March and May 1520, he committed all his ideas to paper – and the text went through eight editions within the same year. A sensation. And that even though in 1520, the Reformer published several other important writings that were also printed in huge numbers. Society had obviously been waiting eagerly for the first Protestant ethic.

This is no surprise. After all, the question of 'good works' was what had given rise to the whole dispute about indulgences. Can man 'do' something for the salvation of his or her soul? 'No,' Luther had declared, 'they cannot, they are justified by God by grace alone'. That meant that from now on the Reformer unambiguously protested against any form of piety based on merit. There is no 'justification by works', no divine favour we could earn by anything we do.

At the same time, though, the Reformation took shape at the end of the Middle Ages – during a period, that is, in which certain expressions of the faith had for centuries been taken for granted. So if it is true that man can contribute nothing to go to heaven – what about fasting and alms, then? Do we even still have to pray? What becomes of the pilgrimages, the calling on the Saints, the spiritual vows and the veneration of relics? And should we continue to fund Masses to be read for the benefit of our departed loved ones?

The Reformers were facing all these questions, and from today's perspective, it is probably hardly possible to imagine the full extent of the changes that were taking place in the spiritual self-image and practice of the people at the time. Everything they had thought of as pious and good since time immemorial was now in question.

Luther decided to take on these insecurities with a fundamental exploration of ethical maxims. It seems to have done him good to be in demand not as a theological revolutionary for a change, but as a pastor. That allowed him to explain carefully and solicitously what the commandments mean for Protestant believers and how they should be dealt with in practice.

The importance of this treatise also lay in the fact that there were all sorts of groups trying to benefit from the people's insecurity for their own purposes. Thus, Luther distanced himself both from moralists and from radical libertarians and laid the foundation for modern Protestant ethics of responsibility.

I have hoped that your princely Grace ... would not despise this my humble offering which I have felt more need of publishing than any other of my sermons or tracts. With this dedication to John, Duke of Saxony, Luther sets the tone: This substantial work is important, for it explains – deliberately in German – how a good Christian should behave, based on the Ten Commandments.

The first commandment:
You shall honour God!
Because God has given the commandments to man and Jesus Christ brings the fulfilment of all commandments, faith in God is the centre of all commandments. *For in this work all good works must be done and receive from it the inflow of their goodness.* In the end, this means that everything done in true faith is a good work – whether in church, at work or at home – *even though they were as insignificant as the picking up of a straw.* And everything done not in faith is sin. After all, in principle even a heathen or a sinner can do good, but only faith makes any act a good work.

That is why there are no more significant or less significant 'good works'. What matters is the love that is in them. As a lover does everything for the well-being of his beloved, a Christian does everything for his or her neighbour. First and foremost, therefore, we should strive to keep the faith, even when we go through bad times or are even haunted by an evil fate. To have one God means to *trust him with the heart, and look to Him for all good, grace and favour, whether in works or sufferings, in life or death, in joy or sorrow.* Failing to do that means to violate the first commandment – and then the deed one does do not matter a bit anymore. That is precisely why the first commandment is the heart of all ethics, and the hardest one to keep. It could even be said that if everyone would keep the first commandment, we would not even need all the others. But as this is not the case, God has developed his good order for the slothful, the sinners and the childish ones.

By the way, people who still ask themselves whether their deeds are good just because they still kick over the traces once in a while, only show that they *still regard faith as a work among other works, and do not set it above all works.*

The second commandment:
You shall honour God's name!
Luther sees clearly that the way someone uses the name of God shows what his faith looks like. *Indeed there is no work in which confidence and faith are so much experienced and felt as in honouring God's Name.* That is why God wants to impress upon us that our whole existence should be one song of praise. It is a difference, after all, whether I keep looking for my own merits or for worldly honour or whether, above all, I praise God for what he is doing.

In short, if someone endeavoured to honour God from morning to evening, they would have their hands full. And anyone who praises God consistently clearly puts him in the centre. Of course, we always should take care of our own honour too, but *this is the correct use of God's Name and honour, when God is thereby praised.*

Anyone who turns directly to God in his need and does not believe he could do something by himself, is honouring God. And of course, we should not make the mistake of swearing or cursing in God's name. Indeed, praising God can consist in openly calling out injustice and speaking *the truth boldly.*

The third commandment:
You shall hallow the day of rest!
When we celebrate the service, it is important that we do it from the heart and not just superficially. *When this faith is rightly present, the heart must be made joyful by the testament, and grow warm and melt in God's love.* That requires inviting sermons and passionate prayers. Instead of prefabricated prayer formulae, people should learn to bring their personal needs and anxieties before God – preferably based on the Ten Commandments – and pray for their neighbours and for the world. Claiming that certain rituals are necessary to even be permitted to pray is *foolish.* We can pray anytime and anywhere. And the best thing is when our prayers encourage us to act accordingly.

So this commandment is not so much about taking breaks from our work but about letting *God alone work in us and that we do nothing of our own with all our powers.* If this attitude leads us to devise spiritual exercises such as fasting and the like which help us overcome our listlessness – why not?

These first three commandments from the first of the two stone tablets Moses received on Mount Sinai now provide the foundation for the other instructions:

The fourth commandment:
You shall honour your father and your mother!
Regarding others with love and confidence also means respecting them. And it means obeying them where that is appropriate. This can only be the case, though, when parents make it their priority to raise their children in the faith. For of course there are mothers and fathers who *are foolish and train their children after the fashion of the world* – seeking only worldly success for their offspring. For Luther, by the way, the Church is a *spiritual mother* who should be obeyed as long as she does not violate the first three commandments. The same is true for the government, which on the one hand is instituted by God, but on the other often acts against its office. If, for example, the authorities would finally do something against gluttony, ostentatiousness and usurious interest, Luther would be glad about it, but the only standard for evaluating the government can and must be the faith.

Luther finds this commandment instructive even for the relations between lord and servants. Where the lords are considerate, the servants should be obedient.

The fifth commandment:
You shall not kill!
Killing is here for Luther the opposite of *meekness* – namely a spiritual meekness that wants only good for

the other person. This meekness enables us to love even our enemies and to want to lead the other person to life and not to death.

The sixth commandment:
You shall not commit adultery!
Again, the Reformer sees a positive value behind this, namely *purity. Each one must watch himself and see what things are needful to him for chastity, in what quantity and how long they help him to be chaste.* And this 'chastity' is not only meant in a sexual sense, but in terms of our whole life.

The seventh commandment:
You shall not steal!
The desirable opposing force here is *benevolence*, which is to be encouraged in all circumstances. Anyone who *trusts God ... and does not doubt that he will always have enough*, will not ling to his money nor take anything away from others.

The eighth commandment:
You shall not bear false witness!
People should strive to tell the *truth*. But as Christ is the truth, in the end it's all about trustingly holding on to the faith.

The ninth and tenth commandments:
You shall not covet!

This, says Luther, does not really require any explanation. We may strive to obey it, but we certainly will not make it. All the same we must remember: As coveting is a condition for the things forbidden in the previous commandments, we should try with all our strength to encourage the love of our neighbour as an opposing force to coveting.

THE ESTATE OF MARRIAGE

In 1522, three years before he himself got married, Martin Luther wrote a tract on marriage and introduced it with the words: 'How I dread preaching on the estate of marriage! I am reluctant to do it.' Which was understandable, considering that he had no idea what he was talking about – being a monk who lived all by himself.

At the same time, the Reformer was faced with the tricky subject of marriage wherever he went. More and more nuns and monks were leaving their monasteries like he had done and had to think about how they would order their lives from now on. The first runaway monk had married a year before, and others were following his example. Furthermore, it was obvious that the long-held assumption that celibacy and the ascetic life were clearly more virtuous than marriage demanded a clarification.

So Luther, still a staunch bachelor, began to write down his thoughts about marriage, never suspecting that he was creating the prototype of the German understanding of family that is still passed on in Protestant churches today. Indeed, it is Luther who puts the ideal image of a Protestant parsonage before the world and shows that there is, in his view, no contradiction between having a family and holding a clerical office. In fact, both belong inseparably together.

Luther's theology of marriage freed the relationship between women and men from many canonical restrictions and emphasized strongly that marriage is the estate God originally intended for all human beings.

Two years after the publication, Katharina von Bora appeared in the Reformer's life – an impetuous, cheerful and very straightforward former nun who, after some confusion, became his wife. Not simply because of passionate love, by the way. Martin Luther was much too cerebral a person for that. But the former monk had not only promised his father to start a family, he also realised, as he writes, that he could not live up to his own standards if he did not practise his teachings in his own life. Thus, his treatise on 'The Estate of Marriage' may have influenced the Reformer's personal choice.

Which he never regretted. For 'Käthe' presided over an exemplary parsonage. People came for meals all the time, the whole family was involved in the father's work, they mostly looked after their own provisions (including brewing their own beer), and faith was in the middle of it all from morning to evening. Even when Luther had the slightest occasion to admonish her, he wrapped it in a spiritual exhortation: 'You want to care instead of God, as if he were not almighty. Leave me alone with your care. I have a better carer than you and all the angels are. Therefore be satisfied. Amen.'

Would Martin have liked to rewrite 'The Estate of Marriage' after experiencing the reality himself? We will never know. What is more important, though, is that Luther never stopped letting out little nuggets of wisdom on marriage, such as this one: 'The wife should see to it that her husband likes to come home, and he should see to it that she does not like to let him leave again.' Sounds good.

....

But timidity is no help in an emergency; I must proceed. I must try to instruct poor bewildered consciences, and take up the matter boldly. And so Luther goes to work. In view of the many inexplicable canonical rules and abuses of his time, he explains how this marriage thing should properly be understood.

1. Who can marry? Well, Luther was a child of his times in this respect – a man and a woman, for *God created man ... male and female he created them. ... He wills to have his excellent handiwork honoured as his divine creation, and not despised.*

2. To what end should one marry? The answer is simple: God *said to them, 'Be fruitful and multiply.'* And just as men cannot change their sex, they should not remain without a partner. *As it is not within my power not to be a man, so it is not my prerogative to be without a woman.* Thus, it makes sense that marriage is oriented towards procreation, because in the end it is about a divine work.

3. Some groups of people, though, are exempted from this: those incapable of marriage and those who prefer to *work on the kingdom of heaven, i. e. the Gospel, and beget spiritual children.* For all others, it is basically a spiritual duty to marry, if only because none of us can get away from our drives.

Apart from a calling to celibacy, though, no earthly vows should keep anyone from marrying. Even monastic vows do not count anymore: *Therefore, priests, monks, and nuns are duty-bound to forsake their vows whenever they find that God's ordinance to produce seed and to multiply is powerful and strong within them.* In other words, if a member of a religious order wants to marry, there is no reason why he or she should not.

Incapable of marriage, by the way, are those who are infertile because of physical defects or have been castrated by others – even if they still feel a sexual desire.

And then there are *those spiritually rich and exalted persons, bridled by the grace of God, who are equipped for marriage by nature and physical capacity and nevertheless voluntarily remain celibate.* These are people who feel no desire for a partner because they prefer to devote their lives to the kingdom of Heaven. But *such persons are rare, not one in a thousand.* That is why we call this form of celibacy a calling.

Unfortunately, though, there are many besides these groups who are not allowed to marry because the canonical rules of the Roman Church prohibit them from conforming to God's work in creation – the divorced for example.

Therefore, in the second part Luther tackles the subject of divorce, which may have three legitimate causes that he can think of: unfitness for marriage, adultery and withdrawal from marital duties. The first ground has been dealt with already, so Luther takes another look at the other two:

Adultery. Here, Luther appeals unambiguously to Jesus's words about divorce and declares: *Here you see that in the case of adultery Christ permits the divorce of husband and wife, so that the innocent person may remarry.* The Bible even mentions with approval that Joseph intended to leave Mary, which implies that in New Testament times, a divorce was principally possible. Of course, however, Luther is not afraid to add that in his opinion, adulterers should be killed.

Withdrawal. *The third case for divorce is that in which one of the parties deprives and avoids the other, refusing to fulfil the conjugal duty or to live with the other person.* And then, Luther minces no words: *Here it is time for the husband to say, 'If you will not, another will; the maid will come if the wife will not.'* At least, though, the husband should admonish his rebellious wife several times and let others know of her stubbornness so that she may possibly give in before he leaves her.

Finally, Luther allows a divorce for those who simply cannot get along with each other and promise to live in chastity in the future. On the other hand, if one partner is unable to fulfil his conjugal duties because of illness, the other of course must hold out with him faithfully. With this, Luther moves on to the third part: the question what characterizes a Christian marriage – by which he does not mean that he wants to talk about the frequency of intercourse.

The Reformer emphasizes that marriage has an incredibly bad name in Germany, but that Christian couples should (contrary to what many secular sources say) recognize God's creation in their partner and therefore should respect the order of creation. *Hold fast first of all to this, that man and woman are the work of God. Keep a tight rein on your heart and your lips; do not criticise his work.*

It can be said very clearly: If we see God's sign in marriage, we can enjoy it with relish, but if we don't, we will soon fret about the challenges of living together. *Now tell me, how can the heart have greater good, joy, and delight than in God, when one is certain that his estate, conduct, and work is pleasing to God?* Someone who knows this can find joy even in distress.

Luther describes very graphically that human reason is not particularly keen on washing nappies, wakeful nights and making beds. But if we consider how much God loves every child, all these arduous things become *golden and noble works.* Even a man who is ridiculed because he is washing nappies with this attitude can know that God is happy with him. Furthermore, no nun and no monk ever do anything as noble as loving parents who care for their children.

So when couples get into trouble, it is because they have the wrong attitude. Partners who know how pleased God is with marriage can live it with relish. As for the more physical details of marital bliss, Luther prefers to say nothing about that in view of his lack of experience and just keep himself to the biblical ideals instead. Which clearly show that marriage is better than fornication, unchastity or unbridled lust. People living without a partner will at some point either be unable to control their drives or get sick.

Furthermore, we should never forget that children are also a spiritual responsibility. For *most certainly father and mother are apostles, bishops, and priests to their children, for it is they who make them acquainted with the gospel.* Luther's hope is that his comments will help overcome the low esteem for marriage. If someone is able to live in chastity – fine. But for the overwhelming majority, a partnership is much better. And if someone says he cannot feed a family, he only shows that he does not trust in God: *God makes children; he will surely also feed them.*

To cut a long story short: Young men should think about getting married at 20, young women at 15 or 18 at the most, despite all objections, *because the estate of marriage is his work, and he preserves in and through the sin all that good which he has implanted and blessed in a marriage.*

TO THE COUNCILMEN OF ALL CITIES IN GERMANY THAT THEY ESTABLISH AND MAINTAIN CHRISTIAN SCHOOLS

Inspired by humanism, the Reformers recognized early on the challenge presented by the lack of education among the people in the late Middle Ages. It was all very well that there was now a German New Testament, but as a sizable portion of the population could not even read, communication was still a problem. How could people be encouraged to develop an autonomous faith and to personally engage with God when they lacked the elementary skills and knowledge to do so?

Furthermore, even in the clerical hierarchy there were massive educational deficiencies at the time. Martin Luther himself was ordained a priest in 1507 – and then decided to study theology. Talk about putting the cart before the donkey! In fact, even many clerics knew little about theology. Some did not even know any Latin. Even in the times of St. Boniface there were reports, for example, about priests who, because of their deficient grasp of the language, baptized people 'in nomine patria et filia et spiritus sanctus' – 'in the name of the fatherland and the daughter and the Holy Spirit'.

But even if many church leaders were unable, before Luther's translation, to read the Scriptures or understand the Latin services, how could they be expected to impart the faith to their congregations? Something had to be done about this. But there was hardly anything to be expected of the clerical authorities in this respect. For Albrecht of Mainz, Luther's main opponent in the debate about indulgences, was both an archbishop and a cardinal – even though he had not had any theological training at all.

The decline of the German school system during the turmoils of the early 16th century did not help matters either. The numbers of university students went down noticeably, while the rise of enthusiastic movements was accompanied by strong anti-intellectual, anti-education tendencies. Which was only understandable: If you are convinced that the Holy Spirit himself proclaims all truth to you, you don't need any education.

Consequently, Martin Luther, and even more Philipp Melanchthon, were urging for a promotion of education. For example, the Reformer from Wittenberg wrote the 'Small' and the 'Large Catechism', a sort of summary of the most important matters of faith for laypeople. Something like a school textbook for believers, as it were. And he kept emphasizing that the Sunday sermons should be leading people to faith in an understandable way too.

Early in 1524, Luther's appeal 'To the Councilmen of All Cities in Germany that they Establish and Maintain

Christian Schools' appeared – printed by Lucas Cranach. In this tract, Luther openly addresses the leadership of the cities and invites them to use their local influence for social progress by promoting an educational reform. This proved to be a very consequential text which led to children hearing about the basic ideas of the Reformation in School, so that future generations were enabled to discover the broad horizons of faith.

....

Let the little children come to me and do not hinder them. Luther starts by quoting Jesus and exhorts the councilmen to do more for education. For it is obvious, says the Reformer, that the devil is using the societal turmoil to keep young people away from education.

But since Moses already mentioned that parents should teach their children, there is a duty especially in this time of upheaval to provide good schooling.

Now one could suppose that education is a task for the biological parents, but for one thing, they are not capable of doing that, and second, many now think that classes are not needed anymore, now that so many monasteries are being dissolved: *I blush ... especially for us Germans, who are such utter blockheads and beasts that we can ask, 'Pray, what good are schools if one is not to become a spiritual?'*

For Luther, however, education is indispensable, regardless of the vocation one wants to pursue. *Alas! I know well that we Germans must always remain brutes and stupid beasts, as neighbouring nations call us.* In other words: The

German school system has a bad reputation abroad too. So it is about time to remember our own virtues.

And those, in Germany, include the humanist educational ideal, which includes the teaching of Latin, Greek, and Hebrew – even if some are critical of that. *Therefore, my beloved Germans, let us open our eyes, thank God for this precious treasure, and guard it well, lest it be again taken from us.* For only because of the good language skills of the German scholars it had been possible to translate the Bible into German. Greek and Hebrew are, after all, the original languages of the Scriptures.

This brings Luther to his main subject: Only those who have mastered the 'sacred' languages will in the future be able to examine whether God's word is being interpreted correctly. *The languages are the sheath in which this sword of the Spirit is contained.* Indeed, people who do not know the ancient languages anymore will get worse and worse at German as well. For example, in monasteries which neglected Greek and Hebrew, it proved that Latin and German were being lost too. *Hence it is certain that unless the languages remain the Gospel must finally perish.* Consequently, it can be said that historically, whenever the ancient languages were neglected, the Gospel was obscured too. Now that they are being promoted, the light of the Gospel is starting to shine again.

Of course, some might point to all those who found salvation without knowing any Greek or Hebrew. Yes, Luther replies, that may be, but even the Early Father St. Augustine made many theological mistakes he could have avoided if he had properly mastered the languages.

Now when men defend the faith with such uncertain arguments and mistaken prooftexts, are not Christians put to shame and made a laughing-stock in the eyes of opponents who know the language? In short, for Luther, it is obvious that the decline of the ancient languages is partly responsible for the crisis of the faith itself.

If the true Gospel is to be protected and promoted, then Hebrew and Greek must be protected and promoted too. Of course, not every little preacher must plough his way through the original text all the time, but anyone who wants to get to the bottom of the Scriptures will not get around knowing the original languages. By way of illustration, the professor from Wittenberg writes: *A Turk's speech must needs be obscure to me; a Turkish child of seven would easily understand him, whereas I do not know the language.* Real understanding of others is only possible if I learn their language. The same is true of the text of the Scriptures.

That is also why it did not make any sense at all for the Church to think for centuries that it could pass on the Gospel mainly through the writings of the Fathers and through pious explanations. *For in comparison with the comments of all the fathers, the languages are as sunlight to shadow.* The theologians that were being cited by the Church all this time would certainly have been glad if they had been offered the opportunity to learn Greek and Hebrew themselves so they could have checked their insights against the original languages. Even the apostle Paul emphasized that all spiritual teaching must be put to the test again and again. But how could one do that without languages? *But in order to judge, men must know the languages, otherwise it is impossible.* Where people can work directly with the original texts of the Old and New Testaments, *faith finds itself constantly renewed.*

Nowadays, however, there are people who claim the Holy Spirit is more important than the Bible. To those, Luther explains unambiguously that it is impossible to play these two off against each other. First of all, he has enough Spirit himself (*perhaps more of it ... than they in all their vaunting shall see in a year*), and second, he would not have been able to confront the papists and all his opponents if the languages had not given him access to the original texts. *The devil has not so much respect for my spirit as he has for my speech and pen when they deal with Scripture.*

Of course, a theologian needs the Holy Spirit, Luther is saying, but then he must be able to properly examine his own spiritual insights. Groups like the Waldensians, who despise the ancient languages, *remain unequipped and unskilled in the defence of the faith against error.* Someone who knows neither Greek nor Latin will in all likelihood frequently lack *the ability to treat Scripture with certainty and thoroughness and to be useful to other nations.*

Thus, Luther encourages the councilmen to press for a type of school that will continue to hold up the humanist ideal of learning the languages. However, in addition to all the spiritual benefits, the new schools should at the same time take care of the physical education – and be places of joy: *The young must romp and leap or at least have something to do that gives them pleasure.*

Therefore, Luther recommends two hours of classes a day. *But the exceptional pupils ... should be kept longer at school or altogether dedicated to a life of study.* For one thing is clear: The greatest kingdoms in history have always been those who invested in education and built great libraries. That should be a model to everyone.

ORDER OF A CHURCH TREASURE, ADVICE HOW TO HANDLE THE SPIRITUAL GOODS

The parish churches that decided to live by Reformatory beliefs in the future soon found themselves face to face with a terrifying reality: How would they be able to sustain themselves financially from now on?

After cutting loose from the mother church, any help from here was hardly to be reckoned with. And all the other sources of revenue that had been so lucrative in the past fell victim to the new teaching as well: No Masses for the dead were being sold anymore, donations on holidays dried up because there was to be no veneration of the Saints anymore, visits by pilgrims at the sites of significant relics were stopped, and even begging was not allowed anymore.

But of course, there were still a lot of bills to be paid. Parsonage, the sexton's quarters, schools, buildings – and above all the care for the elderly. Who was going to pay for all that now? And how? One thing was obvious to all involved – the church finances must be reorganized.

So, Martin Luther, the erudite theologian, had to grapple with entirely worldly, fiscal questions suddenly. For the churches needed guidance how to proceed.

But Luther would not have been Luther if he had not regarded this problem too from a predominantly spiritual perspective. How can we handle finances responsibly while keeping the message of Jesus Christ in mind?

The first attempt to tackle the problem was made in Wittenberg itself – in 1521, with the 'Order of the Common Pouch at Wittenberg'. In practice, it worked like this: A donation box was placed in the middle of the church, and every Sunday the mayor of Wittenberg, together with four assistants chosen by him, removed the money from it and distributed it to the needy as he saw fit. An early form of voluntary contribution to social security, as it were.

It would certainly have been interesting to listen in to one of these distribution meetings, but there was no discernible theological concept behind it as yet. Then 1523, a church goes in ahead of Luther, namely, the city of Leisnig on the Freiberger Mulde. Leisnig had to publicly order its finances to resist the patronage rights of the local Cistercian monastery. The young Protestant churches were vulnerable as long as they did not produce a 'budget'.

Luther adopted the order from Leisnig (which is why it is also known as 'Leisniger Kastenordnung') and published it with a preface of his own, which we will look at now. Afterwards, the Reformer to his annoyance had to wait for six years while the Elector took his time to approve the suggestions.

The significance for the future of this 'Order of a Church Treasure, Advice how to Handle the Spiritual Goods', though, lies not so much in the way the money is handled as in the insight that welfare work is an indispensable part of the character of the Protestant faith. Thus, what we see here is the birth hour of Protestant social work.

....

Martin Luther, preacher, to all Christians in the congregation of Leisnig, my dear Sirs and Brethren in Christ: Grace and Peace from God the Father and our Saviour Jesus Christ.

Dear Sirs and Brethren, since the Father of all mercies has called you as well as others to the fellowship of the Gospel, ... and since the riches of the knowledge of Christ have wrought so mightily among you that you have adopted a new ... common chest, after the example of the apostles: I have seen fit to print and publish this ordinance.

Thus begins Luther's preface, and he goes on to emphasize his hope that many congregations will follow their example – even though some criticism is soon to be expected. Instead of the ordinance below, though, his preface focuses on the question how the monasteries' assets should be dealt with in the future.

You can tell that the situation weighs heavily on the Reformer. Church institutions are being dissolved everywhere, and so far, no one seems to know how to dispose of the properties belonging to them. In

Bohemia people even start looting, and to Luther's irritation the looters appeal to his name. Therefore, he distances himself right at the beginning from all those who are greedily hoping to enrich themselves during the upheaval – not without making it clear that probably only a few will follow his advice.

As he proceeds, it also becomes clear that there are specific cases behind many of the suggestions he makes – such as the question how to provide for the needs of nuns and monks whose monastic communities become shaky overnight. The present challenges are so great that Luther declares: *It would indeed be well if no rural monasteries, such as those of the Benedictines, Cistercians, Celestines, and the like, had ever appeared upon earth.* But they do exist, and something must be done about them.

Therefore, Luther's first step is to formulate his basic recommendations for dealing with monastic communities: All those who want to leave them should be let go in peace, and the monasteries should be closed or, where that is not an option, should not take in any new people, if possible, so that the problem will take care of itself in time. And those who voluntarily stay should be treated with kindness: *We must remember, too, that these persons drifted into this estate in consequence of the generally prevailing blindness and error, and that they have not learned a trade by which they might support themselves.* Therefore, it is a task for the authorities to provide for the members of religious orders.

Where the property of a monastery falls to the authorities, these should pay not only for the livelihood of those who stay, but also give a sort of dowry to those who leave, as they are leaving *their lifelong livelihood* and often have brought money in when they entered. Only afterwards should the money be paid into a common chest, which to Martin Luther makes the most sense of all. *But the third way is the best, namely, to devote all remaining possessions to the common fund of a common chest, out of which gifts and loans might be made, in Christian love, to all the needy in the land.*

This is appropriate, not just because many donors' intention was to do something for the common good anyway, but also because welfare work is a spiritual task: *There is no better service of God than Christian love, which helps and serves the needy.*

Specifically, the Reformer goes on to mention that donations should be returned if the donors' heirs are needy. But only then. And Luther himself realizes that probably all heirs will emphasize their neediness. But in such cases, he says, you cannot stick to any rules and regulations, but must act according to Christian love, carefully examining every individual case and, where in doubt, appeal to people's conscience: *Let everyone examine himself to see what he should take for his own needs and what he should leave for the common chest.*

Continuing, Luther goes into fine detail, e. g. when he specifically describes how to deal with the property of bishoprics or cathedral chapters. Here, too, he emphasizes that the welfare aspect should always be the priority. As the bishops of the papists really are nothing but worldly rulers, there is no reason why their property should not go into the common chest. Prebends and fiefs, though, should remain with the current holders to protect their rights until they fall to the community in the next generation.

The Reformer wants nothing to do with donations that were understood as a kind of loan and had to be ransomed at usurious interest. *Such possessions would have to be separated first of all, like leprosy, from those possessions which consist of simple bequests.* In such cases, those who suffered damage by the usury are to be compensated first; then the rest should flow into the common chest.

Finally, there is the tiresome question what should be done with the buildings. Well, says Luther, *mendicant houses within cities might be converted into good schools for boys and girls*, which might prove to be quite an asset, considering the high educational ideal of the Reformers. Alternatively, it might be considered to use them as living quarters.

And even when talking about this subject, it becomes clear that there obviously have been discussions going into that direction already, for the professor expressly states that there is no need to worry about the fact that these former monastic buildings were once consecrated: *The fact that they were consecrated by bishops should not stand in the way of this, for God knows nothing of such consecrations.*

To summarize, Luther mentions that a transfer of monastic properties into a common chest would not only promote responsibility and the care for the poor, but do away with three deplorable things at once: first, begging, which often caused harm, *second ... the horrible abuse of the ban* (which meant that people were excommunicated because of debt), *which serves no other purpose than to torture the people in the interest of the possessions of priests and monks*, and third the aforementioned usury the church was involved in everywhere.

At the very end, Luther, meekly yet full of hope, writes: *I am content if one or two follow me or would at least like to follow me. ... I have done what I can and what I am in duty bound to do. God help us all to take the right course and to remain firm. Amen.*

SPEECH AT THE DIET
OF WORMS

....

'Here I stand. I can do no other. God help me! Amen.'
This is what Luther is said to have told the dignitaries
at the Diet of Worms to their faces. Except he didn't. At
least not quite in these words. The records of the court
officials preserved these words: 'I neither can nor will
retract anything; for it cannot be either safe or honest
for Christian to speak against his conscience. God help
me! Amen.'

And as, although there are several letters in which
Luther gives an account of his experiences in Worms
to his friends and fellow campaigners, no actual record
exists of the speech from the Reformer's own hand, the
'Speech at the Diet of Worms' is the only text we can
only approach through secondary sources. No matter.
It can be assumed that in view of the turmoil caused
by Luther's visit, the writers recorded the speech fairly
accurately. Besides, there were many princes present in
the room who were very sympathetic toward the Reformer – they would have objected to any errors.

Which they did, by the way. The newly elected Emperor Charles V, only 21 years old and speaking neither

German nor Latin, later had the brilliant thought to antedate his 'Reichsacht' (which made Luther an outlaw). Well, he got in a lot of trouble for that.

Let us take another quick look into the room where the negotiations took place. Luther is led forward and bidden to retract his writings. According to his account, it went down like this: 'Now all my books lay side by side on a bench. Where they might have gotten them, I did not know. Then I said: Most Gracious Emperor, Gracious Princes and Lords, this is an important and high matter, I cannot answer now, I ask to give me time to prepare.'

That was a risk, as nobody knew whether the assurance of safe conduct would be honoured. And a night spent in an overcrowded inn was the perfect opportunity to quietly get rid of an annoying troublemaker. Nevertheless, Luther asked for a deferment, worked through the night, and on April 18, 1521, presented his most important Reformatory ideas once again in a concentrated form. And not just in German, but probably in Latin too – despite the stale air and the tense atmosphere.

This speech made world history because here a little recalcitrant monk claimed the right to his own opinion for himself (and for every human being). For many historians, this marks the end of the Middle Ages – and the beginning of the age of freedom of thought and conscience, of reason and democracy.

Not that the negotiations on that day brought any kind of actual result, by the way. Luther was keen on getting away as quickly as possible, most of the representatives of the estates of the realm were fuming, and a further reconciliatory talk ended without success as Pope and Emperor did not want to discuss anything at all but were simply expecting an unconditional capitulation.

But that is precisely what they did not get. Even though Luther had to go into hiding on the Wartburg for a while – the time of renewal had begun.

....

Most Serene Emperor, Illustrious Princes, Gracious Lords: this day I appear before you in all humility, according to your command, and I implore your majesty and your august highnesses, by the mercies of God, to listen with favour to the defence of a cause which I am well assured is just and right. I ask pardon, if by reason of my ignorance, I am wanting in the manners that befit a court; for I have not been brought up in king's palaces, but in the seclusion of a cloister.

Quite a lot of flattery for a revolutionary. But such was the court etiquette of the time. And Luther probably already suspects what an imposition the things he has to say will be for those present. He must have thought that a little show of humility could not hurt.

The Reformer starts by referring back to the questions posed to him the day before: whether books on the bench were his and whether he was ready to retract them.

'Yes,' he now declares, 'these writings are mine, *except so far as they may have been altered or interpolated by the craft or officiousness of opponents.*' Regarding the second question, though, he continues, it is important that his works are comprised of very different literary genres. For example, he has written many devotional books which are simply about right belief and the right way to live. Even his opponents have acknowledged that these books are worth reading for Christians. Therefore, it would make no sense to retract such texts. *I alone, of all men living, should be abandoning truths approved by the unanimous voice of friends and enemies.*

What a brilliant rhetorical move! His very first argument makes it clear that the sweeping demand to 're-tract everything' is obviously nonsensical.

Then, the Reformer turns to the next category of his works: those writings that attack the papacy and its followers because their *false doctrines, irregular lives, and scandalous examples afflict the Christian world, and ruin the bodies and souls of men.* And then he strikes hard: No one can deny or ignore, he says, *that the laws and human doctrines of the popes entangle, vex, and distress the consciences of the faithful.* Luther appeals to the anti-Roman resentment that has long been present in the population as well as in the ruling class and clever turns it to his advantage. In a nutshell, he is saying: 'You all are dissatisfied with the way the papists conduct themselves, are you not? So it cannot be fundamentally wrong for me to call out these deficiencies.'

And so, the stubborn theologian from Wittenberg draws the conclusion: *If I were to revoke what I have written on that subject, what should I do but strengthen this tyranny, and open a wider door to so many and flagrant impieties?*

This is strong stuff, even for the late Middle Ages, when people were not mincing their words as a rule. For even though Luther is referring to defects of the Roman Church that were visible everywhere, every one of those present knew that he is calling the system of 'papacy' into question in principle.

And so he comes to the third category of books, namely those he had written against his opponents. And here he seems, at first, to relent: *I freely confess that I may have attacked such persons with more violence than was consistent with my profession as an ecclesiastic: I do not think of myself as a saint.*

But still, Luther makes it unambiguously clear that he cannot retract even these writings, as his opponents might otherwise claim that he had agreed with them.

And now comes the second brilliant rhetorical move in this speech: The Reformer simply turns the burden of proof around and challenges those who seriously believed he would buckle under in the face of their power. For Luther asks those present to prove to him that he is erring. And he cites as his model none other than Jesus himself, who had said to the High Priest: 'If I have spoken evil, bear witness against me.' So if the Son of God could demand proof from the spiritual leader of his time, this must be a biblically legitimate thing to do.

And so, Luther can be entirely humble again as he continues: *Therefore, most serene emperor, and you illustrious princes, and all, whether high or low, who hear me, I implore you by the mercies of God to prove to me by the writings of the prophets and apostles that I am in error. As soon as I shall be convinced, I will instantly retract all my errors, and will myself be the first to seize my writings, and commit them to the flames.*

And there they sat, those high and mighty lords. This was not going as they had envisioned. Although that impertinent fellow in his habit had said he was, in principle, willing to retract, he demanded that they had to debate the issues first. And that is the point where a historical paradigm shift is taking place: Where hitherto power decided everything, Luther now demands to put arguments over power. Discussion over institution. Mind over hierarchy. Logic over force. Luther reinforces this by professing his commitment to a culture of disputation: *I rejoice exceedingly to see the Gospel this day, as of old, a cause of disturbance and disagreement.* In other words, finally we are wrestling over truth – instead of someone just standing there and claiming to have it.

With this, the Reformer ends his speech. Albeit not without addressing the young Emperor personally once more: As the Bible offers plenty of examples of kings and rulers who went down the wrong road, he hopes that Charles will not *permit the hatred of my enemies to rain upon me an indignation I have not deserved.*

The highlight of this speech is the following summary of what has been said: *I cannot submit my faith either to the pope or to the council, because it is as clear as noonday that they have fallen into error and even into glaring inconsistency with themselves. If, then, I am not convinced by proof from Holy Scripture, or by cogent reasons, if I am not satisfied by the very text I have cited, and if my judgment is not in this way brought into subjection to God's word, I neither can nor will retract anything.*

This appeal to his own conscience is another milestone in history. One man puts his own conscience above the authority of Pope and Emperor. Because his conscience seems to him to be a better yardstick to determine truth than any form of hierarchical and institutional power. This marks, at the same time, the discovery of the individual. And Luther emerges from the dispute as the moral victor.

A LOOK FORWARD

So what do Martin Luther's reformatory insights mean for us? In other words, what can we learn from this revolutionary, wild and yet word-friendly monk from the 16th century? To answer this question, I want to leave you with some central ideas from Luther's works – an essence from my summaries, as it were.

Voilà! When Martin Luther got the Reformation moving, all he really thought about was the question, 'Does the Church do what it is supposed to do?' And looking at the clergy of his time, hierarchical and alienated from the people, his answer was an unambiguous 'No, it does not!' So the Church had to be made to rediscover and fulfil its mission as 'Body of Christ'.

Consequently, the bold Reformer started dreaming of a renewed Church at an early stage, a Church that would communicate precisely that liberating 'revelation' he had experienced himself: Man is justified 'by grace alone'. We cannot earn nor buy heaven – and so we need no pope, no priest, no help from the Saints, and no traditional rituals to find peace for our souls. There is really only one thing we need – Jesus Christ. Once we understand this, we can be calmly confident and celebrate life.

This meant that everything that Luther set in motion had to answer to the challenge: Does it help people to grasp the Gospel, the message of God's love, or not? Does it free them – or does it hem them in? And this way of looking at things is as explosive today as it was then. So what are the impulses we can take from that?

It is important to remember that the reason why Luther gives the highest priority to Jesus Christ is that he is searching for a clear guiding principle for his behaviour. Although the professor from Wittenberg regularly declares that salvation is imparted 'by the Scriptures alone', he soon realises that some of his opponents know the Bible as well as he does and are battering him with verses. In other words, without any clear criteria, it was possible even then to use the Bible to argue for or against almost anything.

Therefore, Luther wisely concludes: *If our opponents muster Scripture against Christ, we muster Christ against Scripture.* This means that Christ is the only guiding principle for interpreting any biblical text. And even more: *What ever does not teach Christ is not apostolic, even if St. Peter or St. Paul were teaching it. Or the other way around: Every statement that proclaims Christ to us would be apostolic, even if Judas, Annas, Pilate or Herod were teaching it.* Interesting, isn't it?

Perhaps it would be wise to pose this central Lutheran question to all clerical and social activities: Which of all the things that our churches and church leaders do actually promotes Jesus's message of love and liberty? And which of them hinder it? Well, this is where the rubber meets the road.

Luther himself certainly made this question the foundation of his entire Reformation. And some of the life perspectives that emerged from that are valid to this day.

1. Have the courage to change!

Reformation means incessantly questioning the world and the faith, never being satisfied with what is, but examining whether traditional ways of thinking still apply. In other words, whether *they still drive Christ*, as Luther likes to say. For it is possible, of course, that certain forms and traditions are helpful for promoting the Gospel in one age, but less so when the social circumstances have changed. Unfortunately, even many Protestant nowadays have forgotten that they really belong to a church of change. It is time to rediscover this force of renewal.

2. Respect the individual!

As Luther himself had to go around the Church to find his path to God, he wanted every human being to have the chance to encounter God individually. That is why he developed understandable services, translated the Bible into German, wrote the catechisms as a sort of introduction to faith and promoted education wherever he could. For when it comes to salvation, everyone should be allowed to be their own 'priest' before God. This high regard for the individual who, after all, is also a beloved creature of God, must be stronger than all structures. Or, as Jesus said: 'The law was made for man, not man for the law.' And for 'law' we surely can substitute church, government, morals or work.

3. Discover freedom!

Martin Luther experienced his path above all as a path to freedom. While hitherto he had been a captive of his fears, after his conversion he experienced himself as a liberated person. That is why the Reformer is convinced that someone whose soul has been liberated cannot be knocked down by any human force. Someone who can 'let go' of all earthly things and commit to God is free. That means that we must look closely at ourselves and ask whether our society really produces 'free people'. And are Christians in our churches noticeably more liberated, more cheerful, calmer and more loving in their approach to life – or do they fight even worse?

4. Take responsibility!

Luther's statement 'A Christian is a free lord of all, subject to none', as you know, is followed by an essential second part: 'A Christian is a voluntary servant of all, subject to everyone.' The key word here is 'voluntary'. And this, in the end, sums up Luther's entire ethics: Everyone should see to it in their own contexts that they act in such a way that it *drives Christ*. In short, Luther calls people to take responsibility. They should take care themselves that their conduct is beneficial for the world and their neighbours. A real culture of responsibility, though, needs believers who take responsibility – and at the same time know what 'forgiveness' means.

So that they can confidently say with Luther: *I sin brave-ly, but believe even more bravely.*

A Church taking these concerns of Luther seriously would not only have clear guidelines, but have a rich hope too, for as much as the Reformer deplored the state of the world, he steadfastly believed that God's love is greater than all human cares. Or, as he allegedly once said: *If I knew the world was to end tomorrow, I would still plant an apple tree today.* – I know, he did not really say that, but he could have. After all, he once wrote with respect to the ancient philosopher, Horace: *Even if the whole world should break and crumble, the shattered fragments would hit me as an undaunted man.* Is that not more or less the same thing? At the same time, it is a wonderful testimony of faith. For what could be better than being 'undaunted' even in the face of the biggest challenges?

SOURCES

The Luther quotes are taken from the following works:

Works of Martin Luther. With Introductions and Notes (Volume I).
Philadelphia: A. J. Holman, 1915.

Works of Martin Luther. With Introductions and Notes (Volume II).
Philadelphia: A. J. Holman, 1916.

Works of Martin Luther Vol. 4, The Ages Digital Library,
http://media.sabda.org/alkitab-8/LIBRARY/LUT_WRK4.PDF.

Martin Luther. The Estate of Marriage, 1522. (Translated by
Walther I. Brandt.) https://www.1215.org/lawnotes/misc/
marriage/martin-luther-estate-of-marriage.pdf.

Works of Martin Luther – The German Mass and Order of Service,
http://www.godrules.net/library/luther/NEW1luther_f4.htm.

An Open Letter on Translating, by Martin Luther,
http://www.bible-researcher.com/luther01.html.

*Martin Luther's Speech at the Imperial Diet in Worms (18 April
1521)*, http://www.sjsu.edu/people/james.lindahl/courses/
Hum1B/s3/Luther-Speech-Worms-1521.pdf.